PRODUCT M,
UX PEOPLE
FROM DESIGNING TO THF

MW01093690

Christian Crumlish

 Rosenfeld

NEW YORK   2022

Product Management for UX People
From Designing to Thriving in a Product World
By Christian Crumlish

Rosenfeld Media, LLC

125 Maiden Lane

New York, New York 10038

USA

On the Web: www.rosenfeldmedia.com

Please send errata to: errata@rosenfeldmedia.com

Publisher: Louis Rosenfeld

Managing Editor: Marta Justak

Interior Layout: Danielle Foster

Cover Design: Heads of State

Illustrator: Danielle Foster

Indexer: Marilyn Augst

Proofreader: Sue Boshers

To Briggs, my North Star, who makes everything possible

HOW TO USE THIS BOOK

Who Should Read This Book?

Read this book if you are:

- A UX practitioner or manager considering a transition to product management (or other product leadership roles) for professional or career reasons
- A UX person working on a product team and trying to learn how to function best in that context
- A product manager or product leader who wants to better understand the UX people you work with, what they have to contribute, and how best to leverage their talents

If you're a UX professional, who is curious about product management, you'll learn how your skills apply to a product role and get more insight into whether you might want to pursue this career direction. You will also come away with a better understanding of the worldview and priorities of product managers and how best to collaborate with them and build healthy product development teams.

You'll learn whether the product role really offers you the career advancement or growth you are seeking with the benefit of a clear-eyed assessment of the pros and cons of product management work vs. UX.

If you're unsure of your career plans, you'll come away with a better sense of whether this direction is one you want to pursue. If you are already committed to becoming a product manager or leader, you will have a recipe to follow for preparing yourself and executing the transition.

For people who are already product managers and other tech professionals, you will gain insight into the perspectives of UX designers and managers and will likewise come away with models for how to work with them better and how to build stronger product teams.

What's in This Book?

In this book, you will learn what product management means and what product managers do. You'll get a sense of whether product management sounds like something you want to do yourself. You'll find out exactly which of your hard-won UX skills have prepared you for product work and where the gaps are.

You'll learn how product managers work with engineers and take responsibility for business outcomes. You'll get a sense of how product managers work with data and metrics, how to run experiments, and how to optimize revenue and deal with money.

You will also learn how product and UX practitioners and teams can work effectively together, how to make difficult choices between competing priorities, and how to say No to stakeholder, up to and including your boss. Finally, you'll learn how product management leadership works and how you can become the boss.

What Comes with This Book?

This book's companion website (rosenfeldmedia.com/books/product-management-for-ux-people) contains a blog and additional content. The book's diagrams and other illustrations are available under a Creative Commons license (when possible) for you to download and include in your own presentations. You can find these on Flickr at www.flickr.com/photos/rosenfeldmedia/sets/.

Readers of the book are welcome to join the author's Design in Product community to further discuss these topics. To do so, just sign up at https://designinproduct.typeform.com/to/H4PqHsVE.

FREQUENTLY ASKED QUESTIONS

Can I become a product manager and continue to do a lot of design work every day?

Unlikely. Maybe in a small start-up where they need you to do two jobs at once, but product managers are not designers and the day-to-day work of the two roles differs significantly, as explained in Chapter 2, despite the large overlapping areas of shared concern.

Do UX people make good product managers?

They absolutely can. It's no guarantee, but the best product managers I've worked with had a sophisticated understanding of user experience research, strategy, and design principles, an abiding obsession with the needs of customers and other users, and a deep respect for UX practitioners. Chapter 3 identifies some of the key UX strengths the provide a strong foundation for product success.

If I become a PM, will it mean that I can boss around the engineers (finally)?

Not really, but you cannot succeed as a product manager without learning how to effectively organize and focus the efforts of your colleagues on the engineering team. Chapter 4 explains how you can use your UX "superpowers" to become your developers' best ally.

Is "growth hacking" the enemy of good user experience?

Kinda. Certainly the cancerous "growth for its own sake" ethos driven by capitalism and its Silicon Valley derivative, venture capitalism, makes short shrift of most UX ideals, but "growth" itself is not a dirty word. Every organism must learn how to grow if it is to thrive. See Chapter 6 for a rundown on how to optimize your product's growth in a healthy way.

Are product and UX teams always stuck in turf wars?

No, but poorly designed org structures and weakly articulated role responsibilities from leadership are a recipe for conflict, strife, and wasted effort. This is why, whatever side of the table you sit on, you need to negotiate the gray areas and the distinctions between "involved" and "has the final say" for each critical aspect of the work, as discussed in Chapter 9.

How many information architects does a product leadership team need?

At least one, as explained in Chapter 11.

CONTENTS

FOREWORD

There's a particular sparkle I've often seen in the eyes of UX professionals who are considering a pivot to product management. In many cases, this is the sparkle of a redemption narrative in the making: "I'm sick of other product managers not understanding the value and importance of UX, and when I become a product manager, I'll treat my whole team with respect and elevate UX to a more strategic position!"

Cut to a year later, and that sparkle has usually faded. The reality of product management—with its deadlines, estimates, high-stakes decisions, and high-pressure stakeholders—inevitably complicates your best-laid plans and purest ambitions. Slowly but surely, you start to realize why some of the product managers you've worked with were "like that." And, with the right real-world guidance, you are able to navigate the complex realities of product management while building on the user-centric superpowers you developed as a UX person.

Product Management for UX People provides that very guidance. Christian Crumlish has lived through the transition from UX to product management, and is unerringly generous and candid in sharing both his experiences and those of other folks whose work has bridged the worlds of product and UX. Here, you'll find compelling real-world stories of the highs, the lows, and (mostly) the relentless ambiguous middles of product management. And, best of all, you'll learn how your experience as a UX person can help you be the kind of product manager you want to see in the world.

As you read this book, you will experience moments of far-flung inspiration, somber realization, deep reflection, and anxious-yet-steely resolve. If that doesn't capture the day-to-day reality of life as a product manager, I don't know what does.

—Matt LeMay, partner at Sudden Compass and author of *Product Management in Practice* and *Agile for Everybody*

INTRODUCTION

"Why is a product manager telling me what to do?"

Most user experience professionals remember the first time they found themselves working with a product manager: in a meeting—for a new job—at a bigger company—in a different vertical—at a start-up—or for a reorg.

But however it happened, something was new and *different*. Who was this person in the meeting talking about "the product" and speaking for UX?

"That's the product manager, shhh."

One of the designers on your team said they would fill you in later, but gave you this tidbit—it turns out that UX *reports* to product here.

OK, but what does that mean? Who does what? Does this project—no, wait, *product*—manager make the wireframes and then just hand them over to the designers to "color them in" and "make them pretty?"

And who has the final say on the product's user experience?

What even *is* a product manager? These days, that depends on who the person is, where the job is, and how the role is being executed.

Finally, what do UX practitioners need to know about product?

> **NOTE** WHAT PRODUCT MEANS
>
> Product managers tend to use the word *product* (by itself) as a shorthand for *product management*. Shortening it like this is a deliberate choice not to lean into that ambiguous *management* part. The term *product* is also used by itself to denote *product thinking* in general (the entire realm or topic of product stuff, including product design, product development, product marketing, and so on).

Before we plunge in, let's run through the ritual liturgy. How do product and UX relate to each other, how do they work well together, and what is the "correct" relationship between product and UX?

It depends.

OK, with that out of the way, from here on, I'll cite specific examples (thinly disguised if need be, or generalized if it's a ubiquitous pattern) so that you can plot your own mental model for where product fits into the UX worldview (and vice versa).

Let's start by rewinding a bunch of years...

Ten Years Ago I Took This Workshop...

A little over ten years ago, I was a staff interaction designer at Yahoo and curator of the legendary design pattern library there (my business card read *Pattern Detective*). My boss, Erin Malone, was a senior director of UED (user experience design) on the platform design team. Later, I co-authored a book with her on social experience design.

We were presenting at the Information Architecture Summit together that year and when we saw there was a workshop about product management for user experience designers (taught by Jeff Lash and Chris Baum), we both jumped at the chance to sign up, I suspect for similar reasons.

You see, at Yahoo, UED reported to something called "the product org." All the technical work at the company was delivered in collaboration *with* the product sector and the engineering group. These two behemoths were locked in an endless battle for ascendancy that happened at all levels, up and down the line and across the company.

Our platform design team was actually in the tech org, but even there, UED had to work with and accommodate the demands of product management. (In fact, I was vetoed for the first job Erin recruited me to take on by a product manager who worried I was "too senior" and wouldn't be satisfied just cranking out mocks based on his wireframes.)

But more importantly, Yahoo, as a whole, treated user experience design (and research) as an arm of product. This was all new to me. I had cut my teeth in the independent, art-oriented web of the 1990s, building websites for clients in freelance, agency, and consulting contexts. These sites were not products. They sold products, or advertised them, or promoted them. A big part of the appeal of Yahoo was getting closer to making functional experiences for people to engage with and getting out of the business of building microsites and revamping home pages and site navigation for various brick-and-mortar businesses.

So this idea that we were making a product, and that product people governed our work, made a big impression on me, and Jeff and Chris's workshop provided a great opportunity to learn more about the habits and drives of product people. It also left me with the seed of a new passion.

If You Can't Beat 'Em...

Another moment that made a huge impression on me was the day Larry Cornett went from being the VP of User Experience Design for the Yahoo Search product to being the VP of Product for that same team.

"You can do that!?" It was a revelation for me.

It was a few more years before I followed them over to what a lot of UX designers still refer to as "the dark side"—project management.

Did I become one of the oppressors? Do you have to switch teams to get ahead or to influence product strategy? Or can product and UX join forces as "superfriends"? Those are some of the questions I'll cover in this book.

What Exactly Does a Product Manager Do?

If you're not sure what product managers do, you're not alone. Quite a few hiring managers—not to mention entire businesses—are also confused about this job title and what exactly it means. It doesn't help that there are a wide variety of legitimate approaches to product management that tend to emphasize one or another of the constituent proficiencies at the expense of the others.

As confusing as this may seem, there are multiple legitimate approaches to product management in practice today, because the work itself depends so heavily on context. That being said, every product manager has the same core responsibility: value.

Product Management Is Responsible for Value

The product manager is responsible for value, through the coordination and delivery of customer experiences, and for making sure that the experience being delivered to customers (and other stakeholders) provides enough value to be "hired" by the user and developed as a sustainable concern, ideally in service of a broader vision.

OK, but *sustainable* in what sense? It's a broad goal. LinkedIn product lead and social change evangelist B. Pagels-Minor suggested at least one dimension of this: "Something the user values and repeatedly uses." In addition to that, for a system of any kind, business or otherwise, to become sustainable, it needs to find repeatable cycles of inputs and outcomes that literally keep the system going. Some of the inputs, usually those related to people or money, need to be at least steady and consistent, if not growing, Whatever you're building has to keep these cycles flowing.

So think of it this way: any *sustaining value* to the organization is derived by taking a fair share of the value created for the "customer" (or end user, subject, actor, protagonist).

Responsibility for value helps clarify a few roles that are often confused with *product managers: project managers* and *product owners.* Before digging into the building blocks of product management, let's first get those different titles defined and distinguished.

WHAT WE TALK ABOUT WHEN WE TALK ABOUT VALUE

The first person who taught me to focus on "value" as the lodestar of product management was Jay Zaveri, who was my chief product officer at the time, at a start-up called CloudOn, and now runs a product incubator at Social Capital, a VC firm in Palo Alto.

I checked back with him because when people ask what defines value, it's hard to avoid circularity of the "you know it when you see it variety." Some people emphasize value to the whole system vs. monetary value, or value that accrues to the owner of the organization alone. However, Jay put it this way: "*Value* is something special that a person or customer experiences that never existed in the same way for them in the past—it's a product that is useful, usable, and desirable. *Value* fulfills a deep need, desire, or want for the customer that they did not even know existed. It's apparent when something is technologically differentiated ('cheaper, faster, better'), abundantly available ('accessible in a way that was only available to few before'), and changes human behavior (in a way that is beneficial to the person or customer)."

When asked who gets this value, he said, "I think people get confused by adding financial metrics as value metrics. Some of those are necessary, but not sufficient, and some are pure garbage. No true value is created by just financial and growth metrics; in fact, we now know there are serious unintended consequences if you are focused only on them. Nothing beats staying focused on true value to your customer—everyone wins!"

A Product Manager Is *Not* a Project Manager

Product managers are frequently mixed up with *project managers*. Even people who know the difference will occasionally confuse them in speech. Abbreviations are no help, as both are commonly referred to as *PMs* with only context making the meaning clear. (Sometimes that context is "this company doesn't have any project managers" or vice versa; other times, it's based on the speaker, the team, and the conversation itself.)

> **NOTE** IN THIS BOOK, *PM* MEANS *PRODUCT MANAGER*
>
> Forget PrM or ProM, too, as potential abbreviations—still no distinguishing characters. And I haven't met anyone yet who wants to go around calling them ProjMs and ProdMs, or PjMs and PdMs for that matter. *In this book, PM stands for product manager.*

To make things worse, project management can be one of the responsibilities of a product manager. PMs care a lot about schedules, know how to read a Gantt chart, strive to keep everything on track, and work to hold everyone to their commitments, but this should only be a sliver of their time and attention.

A project manager is a specialist whose subject matter knowledge helps them excel at understanding the fine points, but whose core expertise is keeping projects on track, on time, and on budget, not on defining the value of a product and driving the strategy to maximize that value.

Some project managers do become product managers and when they do, just as with UX designers, they must master a whole series of adjacent skills beyond "keeping the trains running on time."

Product consultant and author Matt LeMay, co-founder of Sudden Compass, put it this way: "Product managers have both the opportunity and the responsibility to ask 'why?'"

A Product Manager Is *Not* a Product Owner

There are core differences between a product manager and a product owner. Although companies often use the terms indiscriminately to mean the same thing or apply their own meaning, for this book, we'll define them this way:

> A *product manager* orchestrates the efforts of a cross-disciplinary team to ship software experiences as part of accomplishing strategic business goals.

> A *product owner* is a person who shapes and guides the engineering team as they develop software. In this model, they are a bit like a very tactical product manager, but one who is primarily focused on the tracking tasks. This is an engineer-centric role invented in the absence of true product managers.

Originally, the product owner tended to be drawn from the company's engineering pool, and some teams used a specialized scrum master role that required training and certification and focused on the project management dimensions of an Agile scrum development environment. Product owners from the engineering team were often a team lead but not always. However, today, there are many different real-world uses of this title in practice, including teams where the primary business stakeholder is called the *product owner*, or in some government contexts in which the "product owner" is the person ultimately responsible for what the team delivers, more akin to what most businesses would call a *head of product* or what some academic projects would call a *primary investigator.*

Product owner activities likewise are often part of the work of a product manager, to the extent that some businesses even treat the product owner as an entry- or low-level product manager job title, but again this somewhat obscures the origin of the role from outside of the product management tradition.

Where Did Product Managers Come From?

So where did the tradition of a product manager come from? Why does everyone now seem to speak in terms of "products" at all in this digital age, and why are the people called upon to pull it all together called *product managers*?

The deep history of product management came from the 20th century concept of marketing, which emerged as an attempt to really understand a potential customer and to be more scientific about measuring the size of the market, the reach of a product, and so on.

(Some of this should sound familiar, as new generations rediscover these ideas and frame them in terms of research, humans, users, experience, experimentation, or analysis.)

The product metaphor itself is a bit double-edged in the internet age. The value it offers is to help focus and concretize the offering you are building to meet the needs of real people, or do jobs for them, or ease their journeys, and so on.

But the very real need to be specific and clear about what you are making (and what you are not) can easily hide the slippery nature of online products, which differ from their industrial counterparts in two major ways that both fall under the heading of "actually being a service":

- In contrast to physical products in the old "packaged widget in a box on a shelf" sense, most software made these days is SaaS (software as a service), hosted in the cloud, accessible via the web and sometimes with native app clients, and resistant to some of the finite constraints of the manufacturing process (sunk costs, waterfall processes, and limited ability to make affordable changes once the product starts shipping).

- Online products also tend to be services, in the sense of working for or providing assistance to their users in an ongoing way (vs. the concrete experience of using an object or tool).

Regardless of the subtext of the word *product* and the mental frames that may get dragged along by its use, it has emerged as a way of talking about the product or service being built to meet the needs of real people in a valuable way.

A mid-20th century product manager would have usually been someone with a business background, if not a degree in business, and the earliest digital equivalents inherited some of that DNA.

Product Manager as Business Manager

Product management to this day is perceived by most people as a business discipline or practice. Core to the role of the product manager is the *responsibility* for the business case, business strategy, and financial viability of a product.

Unfortunately, this stereotype can be negative: for example, the "suit," the bean-counter, or the boss man who only cares about the bottom line. Yes, there are plenty of people with product titles out there living up to those clichés, but it doesn't have to be that way. UX designers interested in product management can start by embracing the realities, necessities, and even the joy of business. It doesn't have to be a dirty word.

When the product manager role first emerged in large software and other tech companies, it came with that business foundation and was often paired with technology or balanced by engineering and perhaps one or more other pillars (such as clinical expertise in a health enterprise, or editorial content in a media company, etc., depending on the nature of the business).

The equivalent role that emerged at Microsoft at the time was called *program manager*. Today, program management usually refers to a separate discipline dedicated to operational execution of complex programs, generally consisting of multiple ongoing interrelated projects.

These PMs nearly always had MBAs and at times rubbed seasoned engineers and designers the wrong way when "put in charge" directly out of school.

A number of business titles and roles have contributed to how product management is practiced today, and along the way, many people have done product management work under these titles, roles such as business analyst, product marketer, customer success specialist, and others. Execution-related business skills, such as project management, decision-making, strategic alignment, and leadership factor in there somewhere as well.

Sometimes the business aspect of the role is summarized with a saying, "The product manager is the CEO of the product," but this really isn't true. The only value of that expression is that in an extremely broad way it suggests that the PM has a business responsibility for their product that is central and critical. The buck stops with the product manager.

But the expression is frankly more misleading than helpful because CEOs control the budget, CEOs can hire or fire the team, and just about everybody reports ultimately to the CEO. Product managers have business responsibilities, sure, but they do not wield anything like CEO power.

MBA NOT REQUIRED

A couple of years ago, I was part of a team led by Matte Scheinker that was charged with raising the product bar at AOL, which had newly spun off from its disappointing Time/Warner merger and was playing catch-up with a decade-old style of web development. One of the things we did was review and update the HR ladders for product managers and UX designers, indicating what level of accomplishment was required across a series of criteria to be hired at or promoted to each level—from associate to VP (with an individual-contributor track leading to principal, at the director level for designers).

The old grid required the product managers to have an MBA. We removed this. The HR department asked if we could make it "MBA preferred," but we said that this wasn't the case. If anything, we were MBA-neutral. An MBA might help make a PM better at the business side of the role, or it might not. The time spent getting the MBA yielded one set of experiences and contacts, and the equivalent time spent working yielded another. By itself, the degree didn't tell us much; however, we didn't penalize anyone for having an MBA!

Joff Redfern, a VP of Product at Atlassian (and formerly LinkedIn and Facebook) prefers to frame this aspect of the role as thinking like a general manager. It has some of the same limitations in terms of direct authority, but more closely matches the notion of one person with business-related responsibility for a coherent chunk of work.

Clement Kao of Product Manager HQ points out the GMs also have hiring and firing responsibilities, and he prefers to frame these operational and strategic leadership aspects as being "both coaches and janitors."

Alongside this business-focused type of product manager, the turn of the millennium saw some managers and lead developers emerge from engineering departments and take on product management roles, sometimes, at first, in the absence of a true product practice, but more generally as a new career path open to engineering managers.

Product Manager as Marketing Manager

Another antecedent of today's product manager roles lies in the concept of a marketing manager or even a product marketing manager, which is the historic origin of the role in 20th century business practices. Interestingly, the obsession with customer needs that is inherent in product management derives from this fundamental DNA. The obsessions today with addressing markets and achieving product-market fit are other elements of continuity with the marketing orientation of early product management.

Both roles still exist as distinct positions in many organizations. This dichotomy can potentially lead to turf or coordination issues when the product manager wants to approach product/marketing issues from a product-centric point of view and the product marketing manager wants to approach these same issues from a marketing-centric framework.

The article "Product Marketing Manager vs. Product Manager: Where Do You Draw the Line?" (www.productplan.com/learn/product-manager-vs-product-marketing-manager/) does a nice job of delineating these roles and making a case for them being separate, boiling down the essence to this:

- Product management's role is strategic oversight.
- Product marketing's role is message creation.

Product Manager as Engineering Manager

Given that the context of all of this is software and technology, science and engineering, on some level any product manager in the internet age is a technical product manager, at least in the eyes of people who don't work in tech. (In practice, roles defined as *technical product managers* almost always require a computer science or analytical or subject matter expertise with the specific technical approach of the business.)

Engineers with big-picture skills (such as technical design and architecture), a vision for the purpose and value of what the team is building, and the ability to debate pros and cons with other stakeholders to make the case for a specific direction, may find they have greater leverage and ability to steer the ship as product managers.

The influx of engineer-trained PMs into the field started rebalancing the mix of skills expected from product people, with the business sense still a core orientation and now coupled with a deep mastery of the technical issues involved in software development.

When the role is literally advertised as a "technical product manager" or at an engineering-led company such as Google or any of its many imitators, the job application will include several technical interviews involving puzzles and problem-solving questions very similar to the ones presented to programmers, without necessarily requiring them to write any code.

Questions involving sorting, efficiency, algorithmic complexity, etc. reflect product cultures that are heavily centered on engineering skill sets, experience, and frames of reference.

Google is famous both for making product managers "earn" engineering resources and buy in. There's no guarantee that producing a spec means anyone will build it for you. But Google is also famous for cultivating and empowering product managers. The Associate Product Manager program with its structured training and rotation that Marissa Mayer pioneered there has been widely imitated at other aspiring tech giants.

But again, the type of product manager favored in shops with Google or Google-adjacent cultures tends to be highly technical, hence these brain-teaser type interview sessions that really only make sense as a filter for programming-capable minds and not so much as the far-fetched notion that the PM will routinely debate the "big-O complexity" of several competing algorithmic approaches.

NOTE THE TECHNICAL PM INTERVIEW

I still fondly recall a day I spent on the Google campus being interviewed and taken to lunch by a sequence of 11 white men of varying ages and hair colors and degrees of athleticism or geekiness. Many of the interviews were a lot of fun and, to be honest, I've always liked puzzles, although not so much under pressure with big bucks at stake. They rotate these questions over time so that you can usually find expired examples with a little searching. For example, I was asked at one point how an algorithm might work to efficiently zero in on the correct five-digit passcode on a keypad, given certain rules or constraints about the numbers (to do with repetition, etc.). As I said, it was *almost* fun.

And to be fair, nowadays most decent places that pose challenges like these encourage them to collaborate with you and help you along with your thinking. (If a role like that is your goal and you aren't a computer scientist, there are books to help you cram. More about choosing your career path in Chapter 2, "Do You Want to Be a Product Manager?")

At Yahoo, the product organization was a peer to and equally as powerful as the engineering organization. From the beginning, Yahoo's websites were planned and built by people called *producers* (adopting terminology from media and broadcasting).

Over several years, these jobs gained in complexity and ultimately diverged into two distinct roles, one focused on planning and directing what got built (product managers) and the other doing the actual building (front-end engineers). It actually took some time for the front-end developers to be accepted as peers in the engineering organization, given prejudices at the time against HTML markup and the other front-end languages, but the significance here is that the product role, at least at one of the 90s era internet tech companies ("dot coms"), shared a common ancestor with a programming job.

Fast forward to today, and the role is still a highly technical one. A strong UX practitioner is going to take a serious interest in the technology they are designing with and for, just as an artist takes pains to understand their materials, but at the same time the designer is empowered to explore possibilities without constantly bringing to mind the apparent limitations of the existing technical stack and codebase.

Product managers (and not just "technical" product managers), by contrast, must delve even more deeply into the substance and properties and limitations of the technologies being worked with and never really have the luxury of putting those factors to one side. (PMs also spend much more time working directly with engineers than most UX designers do, which creates further pressure to demonstrate a thorough command of the technical factors that figure into any difficult decision.)

The new hybrid eng/biz type product model still left a lot to be desired as practiced, as most companies still follow waterfall and command-and-control software development lifecycle practices, but in the first decade or so of the millennium a few influential practitioners studying what worked well in Silicon Valley started articulating a fresh model of "lean" and "agile" and "fully empowered" product management.

Product Manager as Experimental Explorer

Marty Cagan, a consultant with the Silicon Valley Product Group and author of the book *Inspired*, made a strong case for empowering the product team to investigate problem spaces, conduct discovery processes, meet customers and prospects face-to-face, and seek to deeply understand what people need and what they will love to bring valuable products to the market.

Rich Mironov, a product consultant who advises companies, takes interim product executive roles (he calls this *smoke jumping*) and writes and teaches workshops. They and others have sought to raise the bar and to highlight the most effective techniques, approaches, and mindsets, while remaining clear-eyed and cautionary about the institutional patterns and incentives that can push back against these approaches.

For example, an empowered product team should understand the goals and outcomes it is seeking and be engaged in a process of iterating experimentally toward meeting those goals. The team should be capable of communicating to others what the current snapshot of the plan is, in the form of a roadmap (much more on this to come), expressed in terms of what is underway right now, what is coming up next, and what is expected to come later.

Many leaders in traditional organizations balk when they see a roadmap communicated this way, especially if what they had in mind when they asked to see the roadmap was really a set of firm release dates on which clearly defined features would be delivered and launched.

But committing to deliver a feature on a certain date, based on a fully baked specification, is a recipe for disaster. That process is too brittle and fails in the face of new information, data from users, stakeholders, and changing market conditions, just to name a few.

This is the same notion from the "lean" movement, popularized by Eric Ries's book *The Lean Startup*: The product manager in an empowered team is facilitating a constant cycle that involves learning from what is currently "shipped" and "in the wild," feeding these insights back into renewed discovery processes driven by qualitative inquiry to explore hypotheses and seek understanding, redefinition of the problem space, identification of further opportunities or experiments worth exploring, decisions about what to build or fix next, and shipping to start the cycle anew.

This cycle shown in Figure 1.1 can be modeled in great detail but is most often reduced to "Build, Measure, Learn."

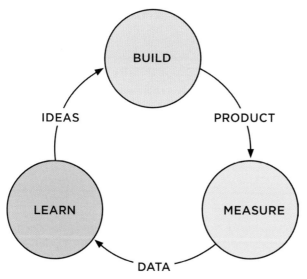

FIGURE 1.1
"Build, measure, learn" is a simple but powerful model that lies at the heart of lean product management, with its bias to action and emphasis on learning and experimentation.

It's worth noting that despite the title and the fact that it's a cycle, you generally do not start with building. You *start* by learning something or by measuring (initially assessing) something, learning about something, and then building a thing.

This process of constant learning, feeding back into discovery, redefinition of problems and opportunities, and iterative design is applicable in the early stages while prototyping new ideas, as well as throughout the life of a product. The approach is still gaining adherents (for example, people like Jeff Gothelf and Josh Seiden have worked hard to bring lean ideas about experimentation to the UX community). Outside of innovative tech companies and start-ups, though, the idea of a product manager as an experimenter (or "mad scientist") is not as fully distributed and accepted.

But all product managers work with data and spend hours every week studying it closely. Whatever the cycle of learning and iteration, the job cannot be done without accurate signals about what is working and how the software is actually being used, and this focus on managing what you can measure carries through all of these strands mentioned so far—business, engineering, and entrepreneurial experimentation.

The most recent archetype to contribute their superpowers to the ideal product manager is one you should be familiar with: the designer.

Product Manager as Creative Artist

The experimental product manager is already more of a creative type than a simple number cruncher or bean counter. This person is someone who is intensely exploring possibilities and looking for ways to discover new solutions to acute problems.

The rise of user experience design in all its various forms, alongside the business-school friendly notion of "design thinking," coincided in the culture with widespread awareness of the creative mythology of the Apple computer, the heroic figure of Steve Jobs, and for design aficionados, Jobs's collaboration with industrial designer Jonathan Ive.

Suddenly, creative founders were getting funding for their own start-ups. Other start-ups were making their first design hires much earlier in the process. Design (or "design thinking") offered proven methods for harnessing creativity and inventing innovative solutions to interesting problems.

Product management evolved as well. At first, PMs paid lip service to UX design, made their own wireframes based on zero research, and asked designers to, more or less, color them in. But now product practitioners take user experience research and design seriously as core disciplines with invaluable, necessary skills and techniques. They also foster mindsets that are required to develop product experiences that people will love and return to again and again.

The lean movement had already shifted its focus emphatically onto the customer (or potential customer). Conveniently user experience research and design revolves around this exact same obsession! UX has methods and traditions for learning from customers, and provides systems and models and tools for exploring and communicating solutions.

Design also excels at redefining problems and questioning prior assumptions, and much like UX design leads, product managers are charged with inspiring and rallying creativity in others. So alongside the business heads, coders, and founder types turning into product managers, some user experience designers, managers, directors, and VPs now jump to the adjacent product track as their careers evolve.

Three Other Traits Shared by All Great Product Managers

Great product managers tend to have the following personality characteristics:

- Curious
- Connecting
- Courageous

They are *curious* almost to the extent of feeling like a busybody, being nosy, wanting to "know all the things," keeping tabs on everything, and being incredibly "high context" and thorough about understanding.

They are *connecting* in the sense of constantly "connecting the dots" to form the big picture, orchestrating the performance, keeping people in the loop, providing the glue or lubrication or the circulatory fluid or whatever metaphor you prefer for the combination of emotional intelligence, "soft skills," and implicit ties that enable teams to thrive and work well.

And they are *courageous* in the sense of being brave enough to take risks, make mistakes, face problems square on, evaluate failures coldly, and learn ferociously from every experience, good or bad. This courageous behavior sets a tone that encourages others to try harder and seek more difficult goals.

So What Does a PM Do?

OK, so now you know what product managers are responsible for (value and focus), where product managers came from (from all over), and what makes a good product manager (business sense, entrepreneurialism, technical chops, experimentalism, creativity, inquisitiveness, emotional intelligence, and courage—easy peasy, right?).

But how does a PM apply that mix of skills and aptitudes to fulfill these responsibilities? What are the primary activities, processes, and tasks of a product manager, or in other words, "What exactly does a PM do all day?"

For a day in the life of a product manager, check out the section "A Typical Day" in Chapter 2, "Do You Want to Be a Product Manager?"

Key Insights

- Product managers are responsible for value. A sufficiently valuable product will delight customers and support the business making the product financially.

- Don't confuse *product* management and *project* management, but product managers do usually have some project management responsibilities.

- A product owner fills a role in Agile scrum development practices and is not the same as a product manager, but some product managers do fill this role as well.

- Product management originated as a business discipline, influenced by product marketing, business analysis, program management, among other practices studied in MBA programs.

- In the software development world, many engineering managers have evolved into product managers.

- In Silicon Valley (writ large), product management has taken on the entrepreneurial virtues of experimentation and exploration, and the "build, measure, learn" cycle.

- Today, it is becoming more common for UX design practitioners and managers to move into product management roles, bringing the creativity and innovation of design crafts with them. (You are here.)

- Great product managers are (benign) busybodies who constantly weave together the motley strands that make up software and are brave enough to lead teams into the unknown in search of insights and ever greater value.

CHAPTER 2

Do You Want to Be a Product Manager?

o far, the role of a product manager probably sounds pretty good. It may be a bit broad and overleveraged at times, but it does play a pivotal role in what actually gets done, potentially expanding the range of influence beyond all but the most influential UX leader.

If you're already practicing UX in the context of a product team, or if you're preparing to transition to a product-oriented organizational model, or being asked to fulfill a quasi-product role in addition to your UX responsibilities, then you've got good reasons for wanting to understand what makes product managers tick and what product management is really all about.

Beyond that lies the idea of fully moving from a UX-defined role to becoming a product manager yourself, full time. Maybe you've started wondering if you want to be a product manager, or even beginning to think that yes, in fact, you do want to be a product manager. If that's part of your reason for picking up this book, then this is a good opportunity to practice the old "Five why's" method of inquiry invented by precocious children, starting with the following basic question: Why do you want to be a product manager?

Why a Product Manager?

Putting aside the challenges involved in doing the job effectively, there are a number of reasons why it might have occurred to you that product management might represent a viable career growth direction for you as a UX practitioner. Some of your reasons might be the following:

Professional and career

- Professional interests
- Career progression planning

Ambition

- Realities of the current org structure
- Lust for power ("the dark side")

Evolving interests

- Waning interest in UX practitioner work
- Fascination with the business side of product

Professional and Career Reasons

UX career paths vary across organizations, for sure, but within the realm of design and related practices, such as user research and UX writing, the most common fork in the road is the matter of becoming a manager of other designers or aspiring to become a principal, leading by example as an individual contributor.

At least in some organizations, there is the possibility of a third path, one that might be thought of more like the "becoming a manager" path, and even less purely about design, which is becoming a product manager at some level and then climbing that ladder.

For example, at Yahoo, before it was subsumed into Verizon, the VP of UED (user experience design) for the search product team, Larry Cornett, moved "up" into the role of VP of Product for that same team. Senior director of UED Luke Wroblewski took on a product role as well. This was the "if you can't beat 'em, join 'em" approach (see Figure 2.1).

FIGURE 2.1

At Yahoo, Larry Cornett (left) and Luke Wroblewski (right) made the leap from user experience to product leadership roles.

So there are times when the organization may steer you in this direction by offering more, better, or richer opportunities on the product track than they do on the UX track. (Another option in such a situation is to fight for better career and professional opportunities for UX practitioners, but it's always worthwhile to assess the realities of a given situation as you assess how best to maneuver through it.)

Take the time to examine these pressures, which are fundamentally external. Be aware of them, but look also to your own internal and intrinsic motivations to make sure that your chosen path aligns with all of them as much as possible.

Ambition

Another driver for some is surely the opportunity to have the final say on some important things. Despite the stereotype of UXers answering every question with "it depends," it can actually be frustrating for many of them to push hard for a strong point of view, stand up for users, make the case for research and design iteration, and still get overruled by someone in a different role who may or may not seem to fully understand the importance of user-centered design.

The urge to become the decider, at least on some things, and the desire to be in the room when important things are being discussed and weighed, can also steer one's thoughts toward product management. This temptation may strike one's UX colleagues as a flirtation with "the dark side," or even a selling out of UX ideals in the service of lust for power (if only).

There is nothing wrong with ambition. Wanting to have a say in things is also reasonable. At the same time, be careful what you wish for. There are two possible unintended consequences of getting more powerful in your org by wearing a product hat:

- You may end up perpetuating an inferior approach to product management that dominates UX but does not use its value wisely.
- You may end up losing what makes work meaningful for you.

Neither of those things will necessarily happen, but if ambition is your sole reason for looking into product roles, the risk is a lot higher.

One side effect that you are guaranteed to experience is the burden of all this decision-making. Like the proverbial dog who caught the car, you'll inevitably at some point feel overwhelmed by the weight of critical decisions landing in your inbox. It comes with the territory. Mind you, some people thrive on it!

44 SIGNS YOU ARE BECOMING A "REAL" PRODUCT MANAGER

In his essay "44 Signs You Are Becoming a Product Manager," John Cutler (head of product research and education at Amplitude) gives a preview of the slings and arrows that go along with the decision-making responsibility of a product manager. He starts by asking "How do you know you're on your way to earning your PM/PO wings? What signals progress? Your first release? Getting 'certified'? Putting together a pretty roadmap?" before saying "No, it's these 44 signs" (reprinted with permission):

1. You'll feel like you are annoying the crap out of your team.

2. You'll find yourself sheepishly asking for an estimate.

3. You'll realize that estimates are worthless, but still be pressured for a "rough sense of timeframe."

4. You'll struggle to explain why your intuition is valid (and be right).

5. You'll struggle to explain why your intuition is valid (and be wrong).

6. You'll be pressured to ship something before it's ready.

7. You'll try to make something perfect when you should have shipped it months ago.

8. You'll face the harsh reality of a usability test.

9. You'll put together the best roadmap in the world, get everyone to buy in, and then everything will change in an instant.

10. You'll forget a seemingly trivial detail that will cause a massive delay.

11. You'll rabbit hole on a seemingly important detail that will cause a massive delay for no apparent customer value.

12. You'll be blamed for being too solution focused.

13. You'll be blamed for being too high level.

14. You'll find out that a new competitor is killing it.

15. You'll have to break crappy news to your team (often admitting that you're to blame).

16. You'll be jealous about _____ and how they do product (and be reminded of that fact because they incessantly blog about it).

continues

17. You'll fancy yourself as technical but be humbled daily.

18. You'll fancy yourself as UX-savvy but be humbled daily.

19. You'll fancy yourself as business-savvy but be humbled daily.

20. You'll say "my team," but feel oddly distant from your team.

21. You'll be worried about "distracting" your team and find yourself not being transparent. And this will come back to haunt you.

22. You'll find yourself parroting something engineers told you and realize just how little you understand.

23. You'll be asked to make your backlog/roadmap more visible, but then be derided when you shift things around.

24. You'll have a day filled with meetings and realize that you added absolutely no value.

25. You'll run a great meeting, and no one will notice.

26. You'll work up a full-fledged wireframe and then try to tell your UX team member that you don't have a design in mind.

27. You'll ship a dud feature that no one uses.

28. You'll ship an awesome feature that no one even notices.

29. You'll have to implement an exec's idea and know it sucks. And then have to live through the success theater that accompanies the release of said idea.

30. You'll try to follow up on the impact of shipped features, but get overwhelmed by the next batch.

31. You'll want to pull your hair out listening to your team debate the technical merits of two, almost identical approaches.

Evolving Interests

As you'll see in Chapter 3, "UX Skills That Carry Over," product work and UX work do exist on a spectrum with some overlap and some gray areas, which tend to be at the strategic, system-level, big-picture, research and data-informed concept model end of the spectrum.

For folks who already prefer that mix of tasks and specialties over the more production-oriented design craft end of the UX spectrum, transferring into product management can represent a way to continue moving in this direction, toward orchestration.

32. You'll advocate for your pet solution against an almost identical team proposed approach.

33. You'll tell a customer "it's on the roadmap" and hear them laugh out loud.

34. You'll say "No" to something just to prove to yourself that you have some influence and a point of view, and then realize that doing that is stupid.

35. You'll say "Yes" to a customer in a moment of pure delusion and then find yourself stubbornly trying to defend a feature that only they will use.

36. You'll hear that you are not technical enough for the role.

37. You'll hear that you are too technical for the role and lack the soft skills.

38. You'll go to a conference and learn about lean startup methodology, and then come back to work and realize that the word *hypothesis* scares the shit out of people.

39. You'll be the single wringable neck.

40. You'll find yourself running cover for your team.

41. You'll find yourself cursing your team under your breath.

42. You'll be empowered on paper, but find yourself taking orders.

43. You'll catch yourself giving orders and learn to empower your team instead.

44. You'll think you've learned from your mistakes, and you'll magically make them again (just to make sure the learning is ingrained).

It's also possible to become more interested in other aspects of making software that don't bear on design as directly, even if they may still keep an intense customer focus. The business aspects of a product manager role rarely impinge on the creative world of user experience research, strategy, and design.

For sure, some UX leads end up getting deeply knowledgeable and wise about the business aspects of the experiences they are responsible for. This can, in turn, lead to well-informed choices down the road about whether to shift to a more business-oriented role, such as a product manager, or to stay in the UX lane and hang onto that knowledge as yet another superpower in your kit.

Others among us are moving through a series of roles. There are engineers who become UX designers and then see in product management a way to combine those aptitudes in a single role.

In many ways, these are the best reasons for exploring a change of role, driven as they are by your internal and intrinsic needs and interests. At the same time, they do not alone guarantee a successful satisfying transition if the organizational support is absent.

So, Are These Good Reasons?

All these reasons are legitimate, and they all come with their own caveats and consequences. You don't need a good reason to explore a potential opportunity for growth. But do take some time to think about the trade-offs and opportunity costs involved in pursuing a product management career or in sticking with user experience.

Look especially closely at whether you are falling for a "grass is greener" fallacy that romanticizes the advantage of the alternative or the road not taken and minimizes the mowing, weeding, and manure spreading that produced your neighbor's green lawn.

In particular, UX practitioners considering the fork in the career path known as *product management* need to understand the day-to-day realities of doing the job.

But What Exactly Do Ya Do Here?

As UX folks start to rub elbows with product people, they become acutely aware of—and possibly even worried about—the gray areas where responsibilities overlap. And, for sure, the two roles do share many values (user-focus, research, iteration, testing/measuring, etc.). These shared concerns can somewhat obscure the ways in which the roles differ, so you should know that the jobs are quite different indeed.

Anybody considering product management as a career should ask themselves three questions, first:

- Do I love spreadsheets?
- Am I a good writer?
- Am I deeply curious about interpersonal dynamics?

Product management is not a design job. It does require some familiarity with design and a deep sensitivity to user experience concerns, but the day-to-day tasks and craft work of product management rarely involve pushing pixels.

There is a bit of diagram-making for sure, and there are a lot of PMs out there making wireframes and even prototypes, but even those folks spend the vast majority of their time working with words and data, not pictures.

So if you love spending your days in Figma or Sketch or Swift, then you might not enjoy giving most or all of that up for the product role and responsibility. Instead of living inside creative art-making software packages, you're likely to spend the bulk of your time using Agile scrum project management tools such as Jira (with Confluence usually), doing things like:

- Writing specification docs
- Decomposing epics into user stories
- Grooming the backlog
- Planning upcoming sprints
- Answering developer questions on tickets
- Reviewing demos and either accepting them or asking for revisions
- Reviewing automatic test data
- Looking at burn-down charts and other visualizations of progress
- Conducting retrospectives

Where else will you spend your time? In email (or Slack, but definitely writing and replying to a lot of messages) and in your calendar software, scheduling meetings that don't interrupt makers from their most productive times of day, facilitating Agile rituals typically on biweekly cadence (planning, daily stand-ups, demos, retrospectives), and reporting to the larger company, leadership, or board, on roadmap updates quarterly, if not monthly.

And that's just the writing part.

You really do have to like numbers, math, analysis, spreadsheets, and databases to be a great product manager. It's a very metric-informed, evidence-based practice. Some of the most valuable signals you get about what to ship next and how the things you've already shipped are faring come in the form of massive waves of data that yield up their insights only through manipulation, reframing, study, and deep familiarity.

For UX designers, the material you work with is the substance of the experience: the words (copy), the visual metaphors, the interactions, and the broader experience. Just as a potter develops a subtle and sophisticated feel for the texture, granularity, and performative properties of their clay, a UX practitioner develops a similar feel for the digital software materials with which they craft affordances.

For product managers, in a very real sense, the material you work with is this welter of data (alongside qualitative signals, of course), which has its own texture, granularity, and informative properties. It requires deep immersion for sustained periods to develop the necessary feel for your own product's data.

A product manager develops very sensitive antennae (or if you're a pop culture enthusiast, call it a spidey sense) that react fast when the morning report on key North Star metrics heralds an unexpected dip in daily active users or a spike in sales. (And that's before even getting into machine learning [ML] and other flavors of artificial intelligence [AI].)

If you love charts, graphs, visualizing multidimensional data, numerical analysis, sleuthing, and "living in your data," then you're going to love product management.

A Typical Day

So, obviously, you know what your days are like now doing UX. Depending on your role, you may spend time conducting and analyzing user interviews and other forms of research and discovery, sketching, exploring, and iterating on design solutions at a high or detailed level, critiquing and reviewing the design work of colleagues, developing and testing prototypes, crafting production ready interfaces, and so on.

You may spend entire days with minimal human communication and maximum time with a drawing package filling your large screen, lost in the creative flow of finding ever more satisfying solutions to challenging problems.

Not all days are the same, but there are recognizable patterns.

Similarly, as a product manager, your workdays will change depending on where you are in the rhythmic development cadence, on the role you play on the team, and on the approach to product management pursued by your organization.

But there are recognizable patterns.

So, for example, across multiple product management roles, here is a generic typical day that would fit many real days across your career.

At home/before the official workday starts:

4:30 a.m.—Wake up in the middle of the night and remember something important that nobody else is tracking. Either jot it down on the night table or get out of bed, move to the home office, and update a Jira ticket or reply to a message before getting some water and going back to sleep. (Maybe answer a few other overnight messages from remote teams first, while you're up.)

6:30 a.m.—Get out of bed, look at Slack on phone, reply to some messages. Do morning routine: coffee, shower, dress, coffee, breakfast, email, Slack, Jira, coffee.

7:30 a.m.—Review daily update of North Star metric data. If anything seems interesting, dig into the source data and try not to lose track of time. If anything turns up that is threatening or promising and immediately actionable, notify other people of the issue and start a process of figuring out how to address it in time.

At work/real workday:

9:00 a.m.—Facilitate daily stand-up with team (developers, sometimes the UX folks but they don't always show up, other contributors), in this case functioning as a de facto PO (product owner):

- You bring the donuts. (Literally, sometimes, and figuratively in the sense product expert Ken Norton has popularized, all the time.)

- Review quickly with each person what was accomplished yesterday (compared with what had been expected), what they expect to work on today, and whether anything is currently blocking their progress.

- Keep the meeting moving, addressing anything that can be clarified right away ("Ankit, can you get Allie the credentials she needs for github?") and tabling other items to follow up on afterward.

9:30 to about 2:30—A patchwork of the following:

- Meetings with other managers (that is, people for whom meetings are productive), often leads of adjacent teams (such as Eng, UX, Sales, and Operations), your own manager, and managers who report to you, if any.

- Communication with customers, potential customers, and other stakeholders.

- Spec writing, roadmap review, backlog grooming, message responding.

- Data analysis, perhaps involving customer feedback, poring over product analytics dashboards, sales forecasts, hardcore profit-and-loss Excel spreadsheets, or periodic reevaluation of progress against OKRs (Objectives and Key Results) or other key performance indicator metrics.

- Lunch eaten at your desk.

2:30 to about 5:30

- Meeting with makers toward the end of their days—these can be regular 1–1s with people who report to you (if any), working meetings with team members to explore and solve problems, or task-based check-ins to track progress, provide guidance, and give support.

- Spec writing, roadmap review, backlog grooming, responding to messages, data analysis.

At home again/after workday:

6:30 to ??—Finally have time to do the following:

- Read long-form industry articles, product craft essays, and reports from colleagues that you can't get to during the workday.
- Work on long-form writing, analysis, and modeling projects without interruptions.
- Try to be present at home with your family and loved ones.
- Check data one more time before going to sleep.

But that's just me, so for the rest of the book, you'll hear from other product managers sharing a typical day in their lives, to give you a broader perspective on the various flavors of product management and environments in which it's practiced.

What If You Don't Want to Be a Product Manager After All?

Whether you came into this merely curious or were on the fence but now you are positive that UX is the life for you and the siren song of product management no longer sounds so sweet, it will still behoove you, as a UX practitioner, to understand product management as well as you possibly can, among the many respected adjacent disciplines you work with. You might even feel relieved that somebody wants to do that part of the work that you appreciate without feeling a desire to do it yourself.

If you're still unsure, the rest of the book should help provide you with information you need to better inform you on that career decision.

And regardless of where you feel you are headed in the long term, you can still derive benefits from absorbing the product frame of mind, one in which you view yourself not just as a UX or user-centered designer but also as a product designer (or researcher, strategist) working alongside PMs and product engineers.

Likewise, if you're one of the many UX folks being pressed into fulfilling some of the nondesign aspects of product work without having (or wanting) a PM title, working either in the absence of PMs, filling in as best you can, or in an organization that distributes more product work to UX people, these insights can prove helpful to you.

So even if you merely seek to understand the product point of view and work more productively with product managers, read on to foster that deeper understanding and better collaboration.

Key Insights

- There are many legitimate reasons for considering a move from UX to product, some of which derive more from external pressures and others that come from internal or intrinsic wants. All come with caveats, and it's worth spending some time to examine your own reasons and look at the pros and cons associated with these factors with clear eyes.

- The most common reasons for switching to product management are a desire for professional and career advancement and a shift in interests ("what gives you joy") in work.

- Product managers spend a lot more time writing and working with numbers than they do drawing screens and diagrams.

- Success as a product manager depends in part on a willingness and ability to become deeply intimate with data. It's hard to do this if that doesn't sound interesting (or even "fun") to you.

- A product manager's typical day looks a lot different from that of a user experience practitioner.

CHAPTER 3

UX Skills That Carry Over

There will always be some overlap between the duties of product managers and UX professionals, but this overlap can function as a healthy tension if addressed forthrightly, or a wasteful turf battle if not.

Many UX designers look at this overlap and wonder how different the two roles really are or need be. For those people who are considering moving into a new role, this raises three important questions:

- Which of my existing skills have equipped me to be a product manager (and will continue to be helpful to me in that new role)?
- Which of my existing skills and expertise will be less relevant or entirely unneeded in a product role?
- What are the new skills and practices I will need to master to complement my foundation in UX?

So, what are the qualities of a UX professional that stand you in good stead as a product leader? It helps first to clarify the boundaries and distinctions between UX and product roles and responsibilities.

You'll also need to dig a bit into the details and get specific about tasks and skills that might be in the domain of a product manager, product designer, or UX practitioner. Something called a *skills histogram* could give you a structured way to investigate these questions in your own context and landscape.

Then, with concepts clarified and the landscape mapped, you can take note of the specific areas of user experience mastery that most directly apply to a product management career.

How PM Differs from UX

The similarities between product and UX design can be deceptive; however, the roles, rituals, and practices of the two disciplines are different in many critical ways.

The biggest and most obvious difference between being a UX practitioner and being a product management professional is in the realm of making decisions.

The Decider

Of course, every role requires decisions and has areas of responsibility where "the buck stops here," and no practice has a monopoly on decisiveness, but in a very real way product management is a role that consists almost entirely of making decisions.

Big decisions (should we build a new feature or fix an existing one?), medium-sized decisions (can we ship what we just built or does it still need more work?), small decisions (is this particular bug a blocker for our next release?), and tiny decisions (does this user story belong above that one in the backlog?) all fall within the realm of the product manager. It's an unending cascade of decisions—decisions all day long from waking to bedtime.

If you're a UX designer who feels like you are sometimes left out when the final decisions are made and your interest in product management has to do solely with wanting to be the one to make more of the decisions, well your gut instinct is not wrong. But a note of caution: *Be careful what you wish for.* Product managers don't get to say "it depends."

FROM THE TRENCHES...

WHO'S THE DECIDER?

UX leader Peter Boersma, who has experience in product management as well, points out that PMs do not make all final decisions. Designers have final say over critical UX choices. Engineers should be responsible for technical architecture decisions, framework choices, and so on. PMs don't have a monopoly on decision-making at all, but at the same time, they make more decisions per hour than any of those other roles.

Still, it's true that on a mature, empowered team, a product manager facilitates decision-making and ensures that decisions get made through consultation and collaboration across adjacent disciplines.

Matt LeMay makes a similar point: "Good product managers are making decisions collaboratively—I've actually seen a number of people transition to PM roles because they want to be "the decider," only to immediately lose the trust of their team by making decisions in a siloed and anti-collaborative way. If anything, I would hope that people coming from the UX side would be sensitive to what it feels like to be excluded from a decision—and would be inclined to be more thoughtful partners in decision-making."

One of the hardest things about taking on the mantle of decision-making is recognizing that it's impossible for all your decisions to be correct. You have to make peace with the fact that you will get some things wrong. Inevitably, you will make decisions that don't pan out, or decisions that make it clear another choice would have been better. As Clement Kao, co-founder of Product Manager HQ, said, "When you don't make a decision, you've actually 'made the decision to delay.' Many entry-level PMs assume 'If I haven't decided yet, then it doesn't count against me,' but putting off a decision is itself a hidden decision with its own consequences."

For some reason, there is a consensus among PMs that even if you're doing well, you're going to make the wrong decision 25–35% of the time. You just have to hope you don't make a company-killing mistake along the way. One good reason why you need to get comfortable with this task was stated by LinkedIn founder, Reid Hoffman, when he said that if you're not a little embarrassed by the product you release, then you waited too long to ship it.

That is, you won't have the luxury to chase down every data point and every conceivable bit of research up to the point of diminishing returns for each decision, not when you're making literally scores of decisions a day.

If anything, modern Agile development processes anticipate this issue with their emphasis on "rough consensus and running code."

One Abstraction Layer from Design

Another big difference between product managers and designers is that product managers are *not* designers!

Good product managers care about design, and the role does involve providing requirements and other materials to help inform design, sometimes guiding designers, and always facilitating the building and implementation of designs. But the last thing a designer wants is a product manager who helpfully does the wireframes or has a few cast-iron ideas about how to design it.

A great product manager will be an advocate for user experience practices and will value and champion design, while being careful not to tread on the domain and prerogatives of the design team.

PRAGMATISM AND SYNTHESIS VS. IDEALISM AND PURITY

When I was senior director of product management at CloudOn, a start-up we subsequently sold to Dropbox, we counted it as a great victory that even our engineering leadership framed many of their arguments about what technical, process, or product decision they favored in terms of what would be best for the user experience.

We knew this verbiage might go no deeper than lip service and might lean heavily on personal opinion about what makes a great experience vs. rigorous user research and testing based insights and so on, but it was still a beachhead in the ongoing dialogue about how best to make software.

At the time, I was running the UX practice as well. It was not just that UX reported to me (as it often does roll up to product leadership in many tech organizations), but at the time I did not have a leader for the team to give me leverage and argue with me about the best way forward.

I was trying to wear both hats, as UX lead and as a product director. I tried to stake out distinct points of view and weigh them against each other, as best I could. But the truth is that—much like playing a card game against yourself—the ability to see both sides collapses the debate, and I always knew what I really thought and wanted to do. I actually craved a strong UX leader to spar with and find the best results.

At one point, in a meeting when once again someone made a case for doing or not doing something or fixing or not fixing something by appealing to the user experience, I caught myself replying "f*** the user experience"—meaning, in short, that we couldn't afford to keep fiddling with the dang thing, and we needed to ship it despite this compromise.

But I did shock myself when I heard myself say that.

The truth is that UX is a role for idealists, purists, seekers, and revolutionaries. Compromise is hard for such folks.

Product managers do not have the luxury of purity or single-minded idealism. They do have ideals. They have values. They have North Star goals, and they have many masters. A big part of product is navigating the path of balance between competing priorities, without losing sight of the mission.

Taking this thought a step further, Matt LeMay emphasizes that "the idea that you need to give up the purity of a single perspective and be able to synthesize and compromise is so important, and it isn't discussed enough," and I really think he's right.

Now it's true that product managers still make diagrams, solve problems, and so on, but if your passion is pushing pixels and your happy place is in Sketch or Figma, then be aware that most product managers spend very little to no time using design software.

If you're the kind of designer who has never feared design management and derives creative satisfaction from deploying a team of talented individuals and bringing out their best work collectively to make something amazing, then taking your hands off the pixel-pushing controls may not feel like deprivation.

UX SUPERPOWER ALERT
SYNTHESIS

Probably the greatest comeuppance I've experienced since becoming a real product authority is that the end result is always something different than what I personally might have shipped had all the decisions been left up to me. No good idea comes out at the other end of the process unchanged, and fortunately I have come to view that as an additive, holistic process where the end result frequently transcends anything I might have imagined on my own. Most practitioners grounded in UX have already mastered synthesizing holistic solutions that address multiple converging forces, needs, and cross-pressures.

Lean into it! This posture will inevitably clash with any one very strong point of view or area of expertise. The sales team, customer support, the CEO, the data reports, the app store reviews, and the roadmap may all be shouting about entirely distinct "Very Important Things" at the same time. As a PM, you have to pick and choose, and you have to sometimes disappoint.

The Day-to-Day Tasks Are Different

Designers spend their days researching, sketching, ideating, critiquing, prototyping, testing, and so on. Design managers do art direction and other design strategy and leadership functions, such as managing the career and professional development of designers and so on.

In contrast, product managers write emails. They send Slack messages. They write spec docs. They write proposals. They write release notes. They groom backlogs. They update roadmaps and present on how the last quarter results went to stakeholders. They talk to customers. They query databases. They consume data reports like water. They lie awake at night worrying about every single thing.

UX vs. Product Skills Histogram

User experience and product management are both "magpie" disciplines. They both draw from multiple sources, are syncretic, and cover a different subset of skills and aptitudes from team to team, and from individual to individual. It can be useful to make a "skills histogram" to assess yourself, direct reports, potential hires, and teams as a whole.

The easiest way to understand a skills histogram is to make one for yourself. First, make a list of the UX skills you are familiar with, and arrange them roughly from the tactical (design craft and practitioner execution) end to the strategic (discovery, systems thinking, and design research) end of the spectrum.

There is no right or wrong list or order. Here is the tactical list I've compiled, which you can also see in Figure 3.1. Your list will vary from the list presented, but it should look similar.

- Branding
- UI system creation
- Front-end development
- Sound and motion
- Visual design
- Conversational design
- Prototyping
- Studio critique and iteration
- Interaction design
- Wireframing
- UX writing

Branding
UI system creation
Front-end development
Sound and motion
Visual design
Conversational design
Prototyping
Studio critique and iteration
Interaction design
Wireframing
UX writing

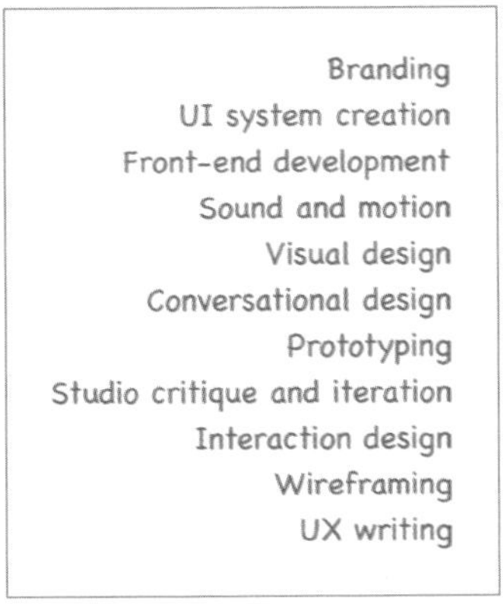

FIGURE 3.1
Don't worry too much about anyone else's opinions about terminology or jargon. Use terms that make sense to you and your coworkers.

After you have your list of craft skills, continue "upstream" or "bigger picture" in the process and finish with a list of UX skills listed here and similar to Figure 3.2.

FIGURE 3.2
One person's single
item is another per-
son's list of three or
four, so again no right
or wrong answers.

UX writing
Content strategy
Service design
Collaborative design
Sketching
Information architecture
UX strategy
Personas and user journeys
User research
Research synthesis
Stakeholder facilitation
Concept modeling
Usability testing

The first or top half of the list are UX skills that are not part of product management. The latter half are UX skills that many product managers are at times responsible for.

- Content strategy
- Service design
- Collaborative design
- Sketching
- Information architecture
- UX strategy

- Personas and user journeys
- User research
- Research synthesis
- Stakeholder facilitation
- Concept modeling
- Usability testing

UX Histogram

Now, assess yourself for each of the skills or areas of expertise. It's OK to eyeball it, but to help with calibrating, use a 9 point scale with these touchpoints:

1—novice

3—beginner

5—competent

7—proficient

9—expert

Rate yourself, and be honest! There's no value in fooling yourself. Remember that you don't need to be an expert in every part of the job to be a good UX practitioner, but if you know where you aren't as strong, you can seek out collaborators with complementary skills, or use this insight to inform your professional development goals.

Figure 3.3 shows an example of my UX histogram.

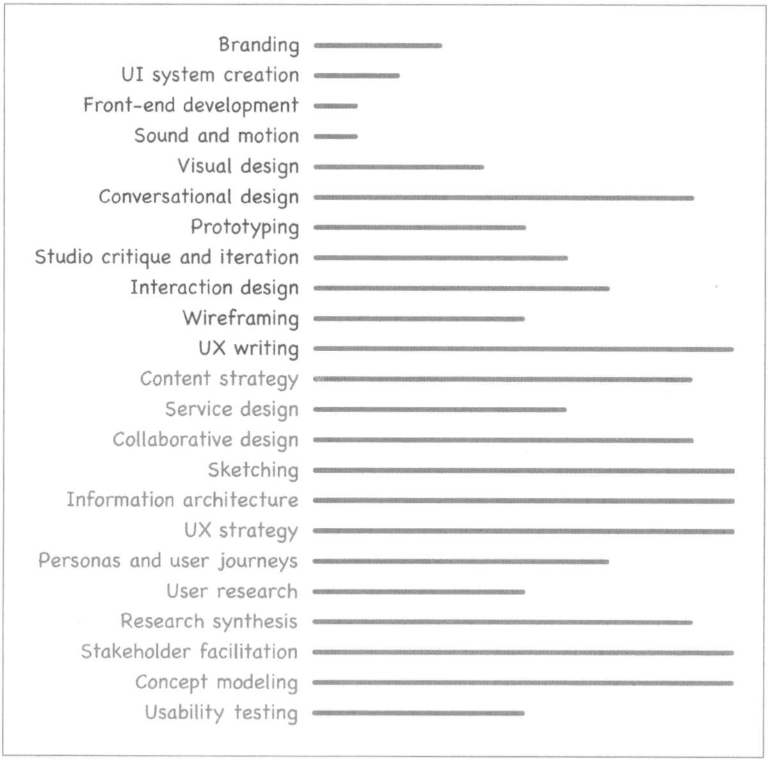

FIGURE 3.3
This UX histogram is skewed toward strategic, consultative, and management activities. What does yours look like? Do you recognize yourself in the mirror?

Product Skills

Now let's talk about the skills that are part of product management, but rarely the responsibility of a UX practitioner.

You can see a working list below and in Figure 3.4.

- Customer interaction
- Market research
- Data analysis
- Sprint planning
- Backlog maintenance
- Bug tracking

- North Star metrics
- Acceptance criteria
- User stories and epics
- Roadmapping
- MVP definition
- Feature prioritization
- Revenue modeling
- Hypotheses and experimentation
- Risk management
- Architecture strategy
- Product-market fit

FIGURE 3.4
As with earlier elements of this list, these items are just one possible set of product skills that might be relevant to your team or context. Your list may vary.

Usability testing
Customer interaction
Market research
Data analysis
Sprint planning
Backlog maintenance
Bug tracking
North Star metrics
Acceptance criteria
User stories and epics
Roadmapping
MVP definition
Feature prioritization
Revenue modeling
Hypotheses and experimentation
Risk management
Architecture strategy
Product-market fit

Now score yourself on these newest items. You can leave lines blank if you haven't encountered them, but give yourself at least a point if you've *worked with* product managers doing these things, or on teams that talked about these matters.

Full disclosure, here is my "full stack" Product/UX histogram (Figure 3.5).

When I look at the skill sets that go into product and user experience practices that I feel I am strongest at today, it makes sense in retrospect at least why I gravitate first toward the strategic/planning end of the UX spectrum and also why I ended up going deeply into product.

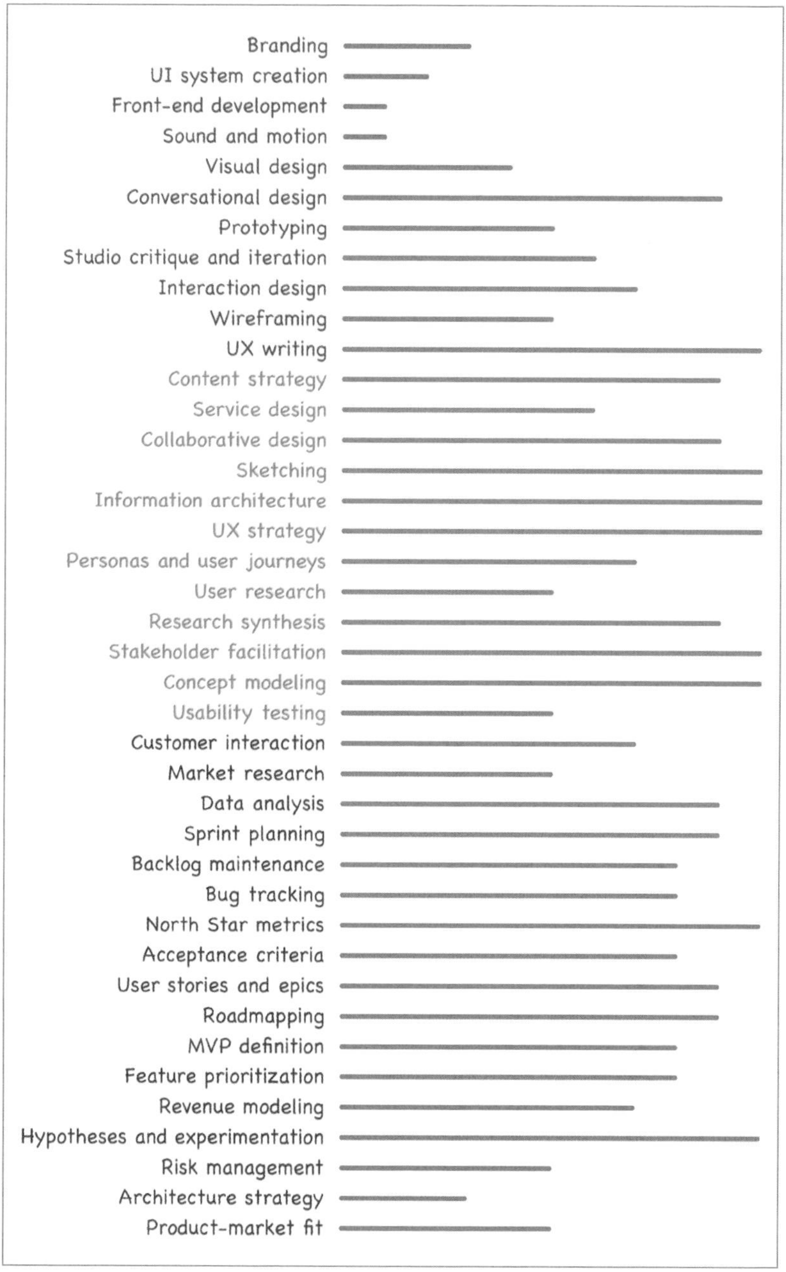

FIGURE 3.5

Here's my self-assessment. Others may disagree!

Product and UX Histogram

So a product histogram would be the skills from the latter two categories in the list, but dropping off most of the design craft (see Figure 3.6).

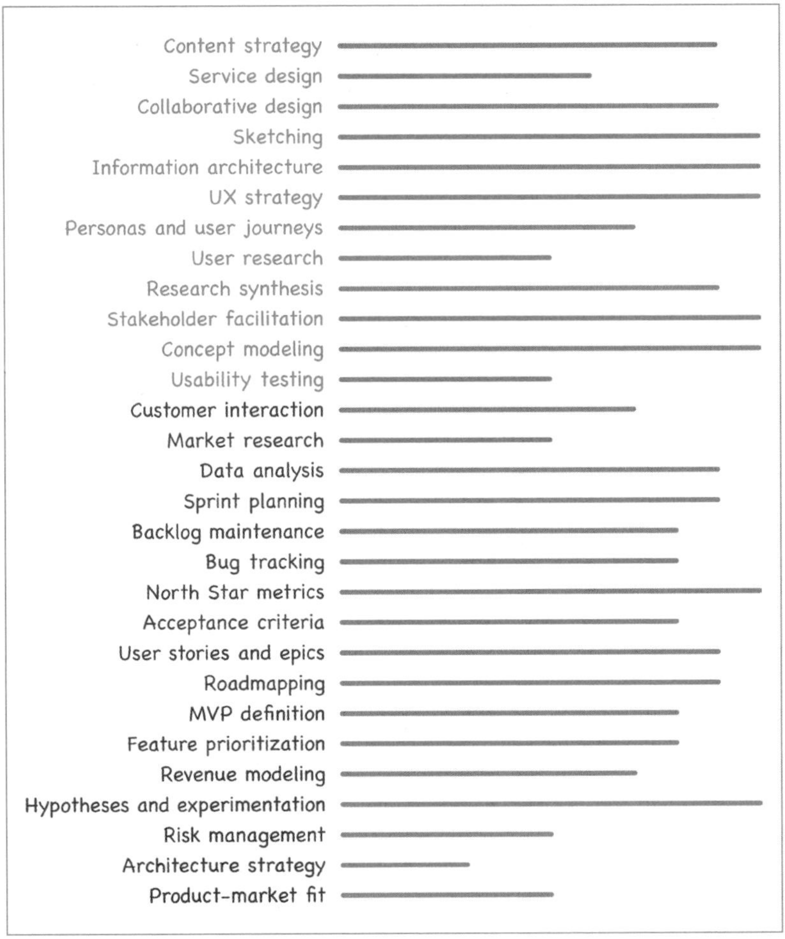

FIGURE 3.6
So this is my product histogram.

If you are a UX or product practitioner, your own histogram can help you explore areas to strengthen, find existing strengths to lean into, select mentors, and recognize the kinds of team you'll grow on.

As a team lead, you can make histograms for each team member and essentially overlay them to see where the team as a whole is strong or weak, needs mentoring, coaching, or augmentation, and even possibly where you are overindexed on some particular skills that are in everybody's comfort zone.

We'll dig into new product management skills for the bulk of this book, but in the rest of this chapter let's look at which of your UX skills and experiences are going to be most useful on a product team. Spoiler alert: I already mentioned that the part of the histogram list that overlaps product and UX is your preexisting sweet spot, but let's dig into the big four as I see it:

- Information architecture
- Intense customer fascination
- Solving problems through iterative design
- Leading through influence

Information Architecture

If there's one core user experience aptitude that applies most directly to product management, it's that oldest of "old skool" practices, information architecture (or IA for short). For some people, IA still just means figuring out sitemaps and the names of navigation menus, but that has always been just the tip of the iceberg.

The critical contribution of information architecture to software design is the mapping of a "meaning layer" that is abstracted from the specifics of the pixels, the bits, the lines of code, the data records, etc. Information architecture provides a toolkit that a product manager can use to forge consensus about the following questions:

- What exactly is it that everyone is getting together to build?
- What is it for?

- Who is it for?
- What does it do—how and why?
- What problem does it solve?
- Where does it fit into the customer's daily journey and how does it provide a better fit for the jobs to be done than the existing ways of doing these things?
- How is it all organized and structured?
- Where is the internal complexity and how is it presented in a more digestible way to various stakeholders who need to interact with the product?

Concept models, architecture, diagrams, user journey, swim lanes, flow diagrams, and even the humble old site maps can function as the sort of edge artifact that multiple disciplines can rally around and use as a blueprint or map of where you are today and where you're headed.

FROM THE TRENCHES...

YOU ARE HERE

Maps make great posters. When you help your team visualize what you're making or how it's supposed to work, you can print it out huge and hang it up on a wall where everyone can see it and talk about it. This is a gift to everyone else of something that you needed anyway.

When I was at the Yahoo Developer Network, we published all of our services in the form of a subway map and gave it out to everyone on our platform. Another time, we brainstormed a concept model for our new open strategy, printed it on a plotter, and hung it in a heavily trafficked hallway near us.

We also attached a magic marker on a string, scribbled on it a bit, and tore the corners some so people would understand that it was a conversation and not a declaration. Once a week or so, we'd consolidate all the latest comments, reroute arrows, stickies, cross-outs, and additions, update the concept model, reflow it, and print it out again for further comment. This practice became almost a game that anyone on the team could play, and since I sat on the other side of the cubicle wall, I got to hear some fascinating debates about the purpose, meaning, and opportunity of our new platform strategy.

The ability to block out information relationships and explore logic and flows in a formalized document that other people can respond to comes in handy in product communication, alignment, and coordination.

IA is a superpower that will aid your own thinking and your ability to rally and persuade your colleagues.

Intense Customer Satisfaction

A concept popularized by the lean start-up movement is "to get outside the building." It demonstrates that you should actively find out what your customers and potential customers want or need or find frustrating, rather than waiting passively for that information. You can learn a lot from product analytics, market research, sentiment analysis, and even customer feedback and customer support reports, but there's no substitute for getting out of your comfort zone and meeting your customers and other stakeholders in their work environments.

On an individual level, product managers are encouraged to commit to contacting a customer outside of work at least once a week, but like so many of these customer-centric practices, they really only work when the organization is committed to ongoing user research and product discovery in general.

Your background in UX should give you a keen understanding of the fundamental role that research plays in user-centered design. Furthermore, if you move into a product manager role, you are going to find a natural ally in the UX researchers in your organization (or, in some cases, you will need to fight to hire user researchers).

There is a risk that product managers will pursue their own rogue research and outreach missions without coordinating with user researchers or other marketing research teams. If this happens, there can be a lot of wasted and duplicated effort, sometimes justified because the questions being asked or the research goals are oriented differently.

However, it's more than worth it to find common ground with anyone else who is talking to real people who use or might use your product. At the very least, ask to piggyback on each other's forays into research, but ideally, work together to develop a shared agenda and make the most of interviews and other research modalities, as a team.

SHARING THE RESEARCH RESPONSIBILITY

This alert comes with a caveat. Your time involved with UX research clearly provides you with superpowers when it comes to techniques for understanding customers. At the same time, sharing the responsibility for product discovery with people who may follow different conventions can be challenging if you aren't willing to make space for approaches that may not seem ideal to you. Maybe you won't be leading the research. Figure out how to make the research as successful as possible, regardless.

Alëna Iouguina wrote a wonderful guide as to how product managers and UX researchers could pair with each other productively, based on her experiences at Shopify.[1] She made the point that the product manager must ultimately act on the insights derived from the research (in a way that the researcher does not) and that the ability to collaborate on shaping the inquiry is the best way to drive research in a productive direction.

Her diagram from this article shows a well-thought-out cycle of ongoing research, learning, launches, and further research, ad infinitum (Figure 3.7).

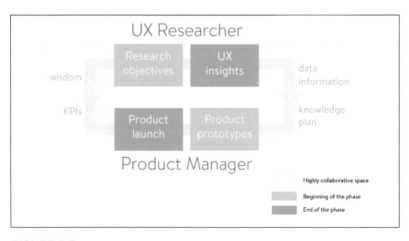

FIGURE 3.7
Alëna Iouguina shared this cycle that shows where the optimal spaces for collaboration occur in the research/launch cycle.

---

1 Check out this article: https://ux.shopify.com/good-things-happen-when-a-product-manager-pairs-with-a-ux-researcher-a88923c94ce8

Solving Problems Through Iterative Design

Now for some of you, this third UX aptitude that applies well to product management may be a bit of a reach. Product management's take on iteration draws a lot more heavily on data-informed experiments than the design-studio model adopted by interactions designers. UX has not made its peace with data in every organization. (Some organizations do not gather data robustly or analyze it rigorously at all, while others silo the data away from the design and creative processes, and still others use data oppressively to dictate design decisions in a manner that leaves UX designers with bad associations for the concept of data in general).

One phrase you may hear thrown about is "data-driven design." Data is not a good driver. (Data, please don't take the wheel. Your dashboard doesn't steer your car.) But data is hugely important for keeping the wheels on the road, the car in its lane, and the destination firmly in sight. So, like many, I prefer to talk about "data-*informed* design." I can't imagine doing UX design or product management the way we used to, almost entirely based on our guts or at best some up-front research and then hit or miss based on what we could gather about some traffic, some clicks, and some sales.

Today, many of us are spoiled. You may have the opportunity to work on well-instrumented products for which you can examine the user pathways and stumbling blocks in an incredibly fine-grained way. We all have so much more information now about *what* is happening, but it's important to remember that these funnels, retention curves, clusters, and so on almost never tell us *why* anything is happening. Fortunately, they do frequently suggest hypotheses that we can explore and test through experimentation.

UX today, in mature organizations, includes using the design toolkit to solve problems and shape experiences to test hypotheses and learn through experimentation which experience works best, which design suits best, and which solution delivers the improved results you're looking for.

So, if you practice UX with that little bit of the scientist (or possibly mad scientist) spirit, combined with the artist's creative ability to harness the unconscious to make leaps and craft novel solutions, then you'll find this experience and sensibility a perfect fit for product management.

If none of these data concepts make sense, then you may have a somewhat larger gap to fill before transitioning to product. So when you work with product managers, you can start by asking to be included in conversations about the data they are reviewing, and interpret what it appears to be telling them about the current designs and their needs and expectations for UX, as they seek to meet further goals.

Leading Through Influence

Over many years of mentoring up-and-coming UX practitioners, I've often found that people are looking for opportunities to become leaders. This is probably the second most common theme I encounter in coaching after "Do I need to become a manager to get promoted?" It's not unusual to hear this desire framed in fairly mundane terms. "How do I get promoted to lead designer?" "How do I become a principal designer?" "How do I get to be in charge?"

My advice usually boils down to telling folks that leadership is usually *demonstrated* rather than *bestowed*. When you are deciding who from a team to promote into a leadership role, the first thing you look for is *who is already leading people?*

Leaders lead and do not wait to be assigned the task of leading. I'm not talking about petty power grabs and declaring yourself to be in charge of things, but more nuanced things like filling voids that need addressing, catching things before they fall, refocusing a meandering meeting to bring it back to the decision to be made, and going to the whiteboard with a marker to clarify the terms of the debate or the details and consequences of two possible logical flows.

Great UX designers lead all the time. They build consensus. They persuade and influence. They marshal arguments and (yes) data. They use their visualization skills to sketch diagrams and models that help communicate and clarify. They surface contradictions and embrace them as design challenges or constraints. They facilitate workshops that get everyone on the same page.

Does any of this sound familiar? These are all things that product managers do.

Product managers are rarely people managers (unless they are product leads managing other product managers). The designers, developers, sales people, data scientists, business analysts, customer success professionals, customer support staff, and the marketing team do not report to the product manager. Setting yourself up as a dictator and trying to just tell everyone else what to do is a nonstarter. A PM leads by persuasion, by influence, and by making everyone else's life easier.

Product Managers Are from Mars...

When UX designers tell me they are thinking about becoming a product manager, one of the things I always try to mention quickly is how different the day-to-day work really tends to be. This may not be obvious immediately, especially since I have been emphasizing the common ground, the shared values, even the small pool of overlapping skills and techniques and concerns, but it's worth noting that the craft work differs greatly. Where designers frequently spend much of their time in various drawing programs or other tools for making prototypes, a product manager typically spends most of the day communicating and consuming information.

I've known some designers with terrible spelling and grammar, almost as a point of pride. They do the visuals. The colors, the proportions, the layout, even the typography, but writing? That's someone else's job. (Of course there are UXs writer and content strategists and so on who already write for a living.) Product managers write a lot—email, specs, more email, Slack messages, user stories, hypotheses, reports, roadmap entries, bug reports, sprint retrospectives, you name it. There's a lot of writing involved.

Once the email is caught up and the spec work is done, there may be some meetings, ideally scheduled in a way that doesn't interrupt the precious "maker time" of designers and programmers. They are acutely aware that meetings count as productivity for you, the PM, but not so much for them.

When you're not writing things down so that anybody who ever encounters it will understand it without reference to any prior knowledge, you'll be facilitating crisp on-point stand-ups. Or kick-offs or working meetings. And when you're not in meetings, you'll spend several hours every day either poring through spreadsheets or MySQL output or analytics package charts and diagrams. And when you're not diving deeply into data, you'll be reading reports, studies, research, articles, and anything else you can get your hands on to feed your insatiable need to make the next round of changes and improvements to your product so that it can continue to grow and progress.

Key Insights

- UX is allowed to say "it depends," but product needs to make a decision.

- Product cares about the user experience and may even direct it in some cases, but doesn't do the design work directly.

- There is a large set of skills that overlap between UX and product, and these can be a good foundation for changing careers. Review your strengths across this spectrum and look for ways to complement and strengthen the weaker areas.

- Information architecture is a product manager superpower that's incredibly useful for articulating and visualizing meaning and relationships and fostering consensus about the shared concerns of the team.

- User researchers are natural allies to product managers, and UX research experience is a good foundation for product work.

- The use of design to develop experiments and test hypotheses and the measurement of design impact through user data and key performance metrics carries over from sophisticated UX design practices to the core day-to-day obsessions of product managers.

- Product managers spend a lot more time with columns of numbers and bulleted lists than they do with the visual design of screens.

CHAPTER 4

Wrangling Engineers

A big part of the product manager's job is providing engineers with everything they need in order to be productive. Sometimes the product manager feels their job is to tell the engineers what to do, but they quickly learn that this is like herding cats. Even with the best of intentions, it's just not the natural way of things.

Your job instead is to provide focus, direction, and meaning and to make sure that goals are clear, requests are well-scoped, and engineers are core participants in the conversation and ideation needed to craft solutions.

Sure, you want people to do things. You give direction, and you should always be willing and able to express a strong point of view, even if you need to come up with one on the spot. But you're not a dictator. Engineers don't report to you, 99% of the time, nor should they.

But they are part of your team, a team you need to nurture and foster and make as productive as possible, so researching problems, defining requirements, and clarifying nuances all help your engineers focus on what they do best. (Motivating, persuading, and rallying them also comes with the territory.)

Also, remember, engineers are makers. Unless they are managers themselves (in which case they are your adjacent colleagues in many things), they are creators who benefit from large stretches of uninterrupted time in which they can summon up complex mental models of the problem, solution, algorithm, or logical issue they are working through.

For this reason, try not to harry engineers with micro-interruptions, but instead focus your communication, feedback, and direction into asynchronous written formats that the developers can review when it suits them and the regular cadences of Agile scrum rituals.

Keep Engineering Teams Aligned

At this point in your UX career, you likely have at least passing familiarity with things like stand-ups and sprints, but you may not have always had them as a routine part of your day or week. Product managers set their clocks by these "rituals," which are formally structured meetings generally focused on syncing and recalibrating, but can also be prospective or retrospective depending on where you are in a given cycle.

These cycles (daily stand-ups, weekly sprint rituals, monthly road-map updates, quarterly planning) are collectively referred to as *cadences* and together represent your primary channel for collaborating with and providing direction to engineers.

Cadences

You can think of these recurring patterns as fractals. You do the same thing over and over again at each scale, and the stakes get higher by an order of magnitude at each longer cadence as well.

For almost every Agile team, the smallest cadence is the daily stand-up (Figure 4.1). Traditionally, this is done standing up to remind everyone that it is a quick check-in and not a detailed working session. Each person reports on what they accomplished since last time, what they plan to get done in the next day, and what, if anything, is blocking their progress.

FIGURE 4.1

Just as it sounds, Agile teams check in once per (working) day to review progress, next steps, and blockers.

Daily stand-up

The daily stand-up is just one of the scrum rituals (from backlog grooming to sprint planning to demo, product acceptance, and retrospective) that takes place during the sprint, which will typically last from two to four weeks (see Figure 4.2).

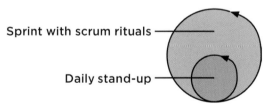

Sprint with scrum rituals

Daily stand-up

FIGURE 4.2

Throughout the sprint, there will be other rituals that take place at the beginning, middle, or end.

Once a month, it's a good idea to review the roadmap to make sure that the Now items are all progressing as planned, the list of Next items is still current and accurate, preparations are being made for when those items move into Now, and all other ideas beyond the current horizon are captured under Later (Figure 4.3).

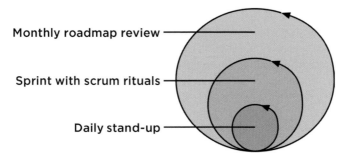

Monthly roadmap review

Sprint with scrum rituals

Daily stand-up

FIGURE 4.3
Because roadmaps may not be formally updated more than once a quarter, it's a good idea to review the roadmap once a month to see if things are on track or drifting.

In addition to monthly roadmap reviews, some companies, such as Intercom, divide each quarter into two six-week chunks with a "wiggle week" in between.

Once a quarter, it's time for the product team, along with all other stakeholders, to review progress against the goals going in from the start, define goals for the quarter ahead, and review progress against the annual plan (Figure 4.4).

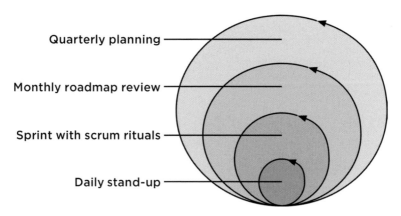

Quarterly planning

Monthly roadmap review

Sprint with scrum rituals

Daily stand-up

FIGURE 4.4
Quarterly planning provides structure for the four to six sprints ahead.

Once a year, you can take stock at how the year went compared with the plans made at the end of the previous year, marvel at how many things occurred that were not anticipated, take those learnings, revisit the vision, mission, 5-, 10- or even 20-year goals, and come up with a working plan for the year ahead (see Figure 4.5).

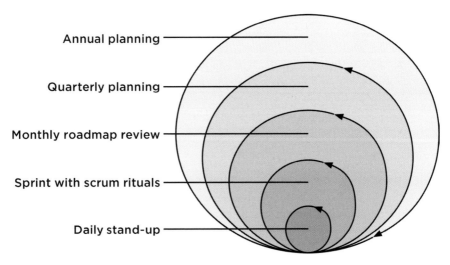

Annual planning

Quarterly planning

Monthly roadmap review

Sprint with scrum rituals

Daily stand-up

FIGURE 4.5
Time for that annual company retreat!

At every level, there are some simple principles at work to help maintain alignment and correct your steering at every scale. Just as the "lean" concept builds on the cornerstone cycle of "build, measure, learn" (repeat), "Agile" practices follow a very similar ethos that boils down to "iterate, review, recalibrate" (repeat), combined with the idea that at every scale your goal should be to complete something that can be reviewed, tested, and either sent back for more changes or accepted.

Threaded throughout Agile principles and practices is this approach to routine course-correction "with a preference to the shorter time-scale" (*Principles Behind the Agile Manifesto*).

Only one of the original twelve Agile principles (the last one) spells out this notion directly, when addressing systematic iterative improvement of team processes over time:

> At regular intervals, the team reflects on how to become more effective, then tunes and adjusts its behavior accordingly.

You find yourself working in a shop that has adopted SAFe® (Scaled Agile Framework® for enterprise). I am sorry to tell you that SAFe® is the devil. It's a corporate set of formal agile-style processes that create what is often called "agilefall," reinventing the waterfall project plan (the exact thing the Agile Manifesto was rebelling against) with the trappings of rigid interpretations of Agile rituals. Having said that, shops that use SAFe® often derive a benefit from the approach as compared with what they replaced it with, and in that sense, it can be viewed as a step in the right direction in the difficult challenge of asking a large corporate enterprise to fully embrace the most difficult aspects of agility.

If you pause a moment to reflect, this is fairly "meta"—it basically takes the power of this deceptively simple idea (of routinely reviewing and course-correcting) and tells you to apply it to how the team itself is working as a whole, and not just to the code getting written and tested.

Very powerful stuff!

Sprint Planning

The hands-on tactical day-to-day world of a product manager revolves around engineering sprints (and, in some dual-track systems, on staggered discovery/UX/design sprints as well). You generally have a very good sense of where you are in the sprint at any given time, and your daily stand-ups should be keeping you abreast of progress, as well as blockers (things that are preventing developers or others from completing their tasks) and nonblocking problems.

Sprint planning is a process and often a meeting for determining which user stories, bug fixes, or other engineering tasks will be scheduled for the sprint about to start. This is a negotiation among all concerned, but primarily between product and engineering.

The candidate issues come from your backlog. An ungroomed backlog is simply a long list of proposed ideas, tasks, wish list items, and so on. They need to be reasonably well specified before they can be considered for a sprint. The process of putting the backlog into a priority order and making sure that the items at the top of the backlog are ready to hand off to an engineer is called *grooming the backlog* (Figure 4.6).

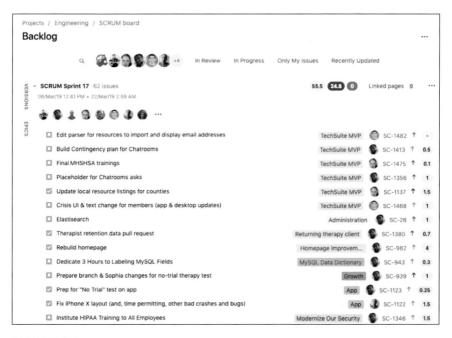

FIGURE 4.6
Many teams manage their backlogs in a project management tool such as Jira (shown here).

There are multiple methods for estimating and scoring effort, and then comparing estimated effort for the desired tasks against the available time and resource budget. Early tries at sprint planning often underestimate overhead, meeting, managerial, and operational time (not to mention setbacks and learning experiences), but within a few cycles most teams get a collective feel for their rough capacity.

During a Sprint

During the sprint, you may need to add new items or demote some to the backlog again. Part of being agile is adapting to changing circumstances, but this can sometimes make it hard to measure actual results vs. plans using such items as burndown charts. The team learns faster if everyone can see clearly the gap between estimates and plans on one side and actual results and outcomes on the other (see Figure 4.7).

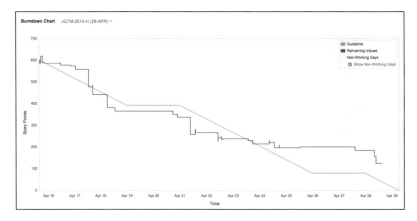

FIGURE 4.7

A sample burndown chart in Jira from Atlassian that shows a sprint going off track near the end.

Many teams use Kanban as a project-management tracking method during sprints. This is a model in which real or virtual sticky notes summarizing user stories or tasks are moved from one column to the next as they progress through the software development workflow (Figure 4.8).

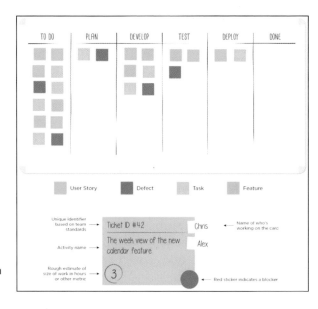

FIGURE 4.8
A prototypical Kanban setup.

When a team is colocated in one physical location, there can be a real Kanban board with sticky notes on it, where everyone can see tasks moving through the workflow (Figure 4.9).

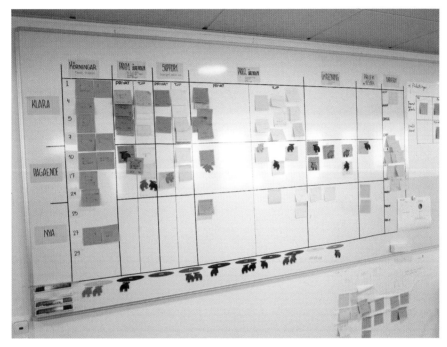

FIGURE 4.9
When a team works together in a shared space, a real physical Kanban board can provide at-a-glance transparency into progress.

But many teams, and not just distributed or remote ones, tend to use Kanban-style software these days. Trello, for example, is a wildly popular Kanban-type software that many product teams swear by, and most of the tools that support sprint-planning and other Agile project management processes now offer a Kanban view (Figure 4.10).

Another aspect of PMing should feel familiar from your UX experience: responding to issues that arise during a sprint. This can be a matter of clarifying a specification, filling in a gap to address an unanticipated scenario (anything from an error case to a clash between requirements that could be resolved in multiple ways), working with the designer to address challenges in implementing the design as delivered, or getting in front of a whiteboard with the developer and others to work through system-level choices.

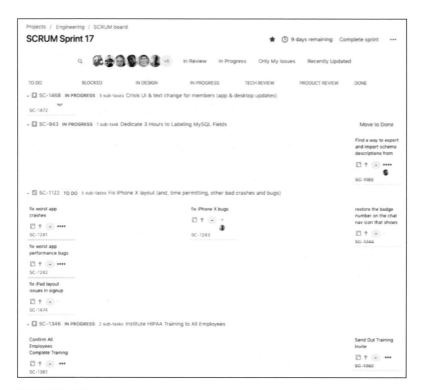

FIGURE 4.10

A Kanban board helps visualize progress across multiple concurrent priorities.

What's Your Definition of "Done"?

A sticking point for many teams making software and trying to be agile about it is how to know when something is done. As you get down into the weeds, there always seems to be more that you could do. There are almost always some bugs that are borderline in terms of not impacting people in very many scenarios and not causing severe inconvenience (usually because there are easy enough work-arounds). There are always some edge cases that the code doesn't handle perfectly yet. There may be long-tail mobile devices that don't pass every test. The closer you look, the more you will see.

But a big part of the product role is making these tough calls, the ones that might go either way, but that if you get too many of them wrong will either delay your project unacceptably or, worse, deliver buggy code and terrible experiences in the interest of keeping to a schedule.

But, again, the product manager is not a dictator. Instead, it's incumbent upon the PM to take responsibility for establishing a "definition of done" that everyone on the team buys into.

This definition usually ties back to the requirements documents that defined the original problem space and specified what the solution needed to achieve to address these problems. If everyone signs off on a definition of done, then it shouldn't be controversial later when a PM needs to say "we can't ship this if some users will lose their data" or "if it doesn't run on Android devices," and so on.

The definition of done also means coded, tested, and accepted. Without clearly defining that a thing isn't done until it has passed through the entire workflow, there is a risk of constant slippage from sprint to sprint as chunks of code are called "done" because they were built before the sprint expired, but they still need to be tested in the next sprint and possibly revamped further, depending on what testing reveals.

Finally, clearly defining what it means for something to be done can help avoid the paralysis of perfectionism. Product management is no job for a perfectionist! Remember the Reid Hoffman line about how if you're not a little bit embarrassed by the product you shipped, then you waited too long to get it out the door?

Product managers have a saying: "Good enough is good enough." It's an excellent reminder that your job is to ship a product that does the job for your customers, solves their problems, and provides them with enough value that they embrace your solution. It's not about winning an award or shipping "bug-free code."

Many product teams find it valuable to schedule a demo day at the end of a sprint. This is a meeting usually open to anyone interested, in which engineers demonstrate the working code they built during the sprint. The demo day can be part of the formal product acceptance ritual by which the PM declares the shipped code accepted or identifies gaps in the form of unmet requirements. It also gives other stakeholders a chance to see progress and a preview of what is coming soon, and to give the developers a moment in the sun after all those hours of coding in front of a screen, often sequestered away from the rest of the company.

Iterative Process Improvement Through Retrospectives

At the end of a sprint, the product manager is responsible for making sure that a final key Agile ritual, the retrospective meeting, takes place in a facilitated way. This retrospective meeting may involve convening and facilitating the retro directly, but even in cases where a product owner or scrum master runs the meeting, the product manager still participates and pays close attention.

The motivation for this ritual comes from that 12th principle of reviewing team processes and improving them constantly. To prepare, the team is asked to reflect on two key questions: "What went well?" and "What can we improve?" and to suggest specific actions that team members might want to take based on what was learned during the sprint just ending.

Using a tool such as EasyRetro, the team can pre-populate a chart with their own items, as well as comment on or vote for each other's items (Figure 4.11). FYI, don't call them *postmortems*, as that's a little bit morbid.

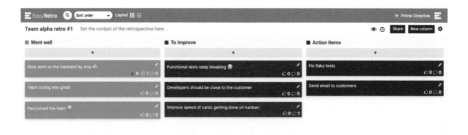

FIGURE 4.11

A retrospective enables the team to celebrate and reinforce effective behaviors and patterns and to reflect on frustrations and setbacks in a constructive way.

The PM should facilitate a non-blame-oriented discussion both reinforcing the reflections on what went well and making space to explore what went wrong and how such matters can be handled better in the future. As team members suggest affirmative steps drawn from those insights, these steps can be voted on and prioritized as well.

When practiced in an open and healthy, supportive way, team retrospectives can spur incredible advances in team cohesion, coordination, and effectiveness.

Getting Results from Engineers

While it's critical to keep the wheels rolling and the trains running, ultimately the scrum-master-ish, product "owner" aspects of the product management job are tactical and task-based. Diligence and experience usually suffice to equip a PM to run sprints and manage a backlog. But none of that addresses the so-called "soft skills" related to people management and bridging cultural divides in multidisciplinary teams where people with different training and inclinations often speak entirely different "business dialects."

Giving Respect

Step one is to show respect for engineers. Respect doesn't mean rolling over for them or taking no for an answer without an explanation. But it may mean dropping the unfortunate attitude some user experience people take that presumes that they and they alone care about the user, about the experience, and about quality, and that the developers are a bunch of unfeeling automata who just want to crank out code and call it a day.

A key way to show respect is to learn the lingo. Design means something different when an engineer is talking about their "technical design" (a document capturing how they plan to implement the product requirements). Lecturing them that they are using the word *design* incorrectly and then giving them ten minutes on the history of design and human factors isn't going to win over anyone.

The UX skills you can and must use are your ability to research and understand the needs and motivations of a person. The experience you are designing in this context is not a software product but *working with you*. If you approach this with humility, you will find that you can meet your engineers more than halfway and present your goals and needs in terms they understand and appreciate.

This will take time, a lot of listening, and a conscious effort to study and understand the "folkways" of people who are different from yourself. Of course, it will help if you are already something of a nerd, geek, or technophile yourself (and let's be honest, you probably are). Lean into that, and you're already halfway there.

NO JOB SHOULD BE BENEATH A PRODUCT MANAGER

Ken Norton, a product consultant, adviser, and educator who was at Google Ventures for many years, crystalized the service aspect of the product role with the mantra "bring the donuts":

"I believe the best product managers are willing to do whatever it takes to help their teams succeed. An important aspect of that is recognizing that PMs often have to do the work that would fall through the cracks otherwise. By definition, that can be grimy, un-fun work: cleaning the bug queue, organizing a document repository, replying to a customer support email. No job should be beneath a product manager. PMs are more humble servants than 'CEOs of the product.' They put their teams first, they do what needs to be done, and they demonstrate that every day.

"In 2005, I was preparing to give a talk at Berkeley's Haas School of Business about product management. I was looking for a rhetorical device to convey this, and I settled on 'bring the donuts.' If PMs don't bring donuts for the team on launch day, who else will? I'm not sure why I picked donuts. At the time, my competitive cycling career was still flourishing, and bagels were more my style. But donuts it was, and the concept stuck.

"If a product manager bears in mind that their role is to do whatever it takes to make the team successful, then they won't go wrong."

Earning Respect

Besides showing respect and humility and a willingness to engage on engineering's terms, a product manager also needs to earn the respect of the developers they work with, if they want to have any hope of guidance and leading the team to a successful outcome. The bar for earning respect may be set higher for product managers who did not come from an engineering background, don't write code, and aren't framed as "technical product managers."

This new-fangled UX design–rooted type of PM therefore needs to stake out some technical bona fides if they're not to be written off as a jumped-up designer who "doesn't really get" technology or programming, just as the business-oriented PMs always have had to do as well.

But how do you establish these bona fides without essentially going back to school and becoming an engineer yourself? You don't do it by pretending to be what you're not or nodding along as if you understand a technical point when you don't. And you won't get there if you're afraid to look ignorant by asking a question.

You do it by asking smart questions. What are smart questions? When in doubt, they are all the questions you authentically have. When you're unclear on terms, ask to clarify them. Show that you have some understanding of what might be meant, but that you want to follow along precisely. The more you engage, the more your own mental model of the technical architecture, logic, approach, coding style, strengths and limitations of libraries, and deep knowledge of the capabilities of your team will deepen and strengthen.

When the time comes to ask for something new or to propose an idea, you'll then be able to ground your requests in the constraints and realities of the technical stack you're working on and avoid something embarrassing, like asking if they can build you a flying pony.

Estimation and Negotiation

You may recall that sprint planning involves estimation, and that the product role requires constant negotiation with your teammates—but it need not feel like haggling in a bazaar. The product manager can set the tone for how differences of opinion and priority are aired and weighed. The product manager should also recognize what inspires the engineers and what frightens them, which can help you read between the lines when they resist something you want to do or when their estimate for the effort required surprises you in some way.

Estimation is a topic unto itself, fraught with frustration and nearly impossible to do really well, but it's a daily requirement of the work and becomes manageable as long as everyone approaches it as a best-effort approach to figuring out where to invest time and resources.

And remember, you are not their boss. (At least, that's true most of the time.) Your job is to inspire and persuade, not to command.

LEARNING HOW YOUR ENGINEERS ESTIMATE

At one point, I had a team of two engineers that I privately thought of as "Jack Sprat and His Wife" because their inclinations were so complementary. One of the engineers, let's call her Cheryl, saw risk everywhere, padded her estimates out of prudence from long experience of how things go wrong if they can and distractions are inevitable, etc. The other engineer, let's call him Edgar, always envisioned a clear path, enthusiastically said yes to everything, and tended to underestimate actual effort by a factor of 4x.

Between the two of them, I could usually get a handle on the likely real effort, and by facilitating discussion among the three of us, I helped mitigate each of their strong inclinations with some balancing considerations. It's not as though they ever talked each other round to adopting a new temperament, mind you, but we managed to soften some of the edges.

And there is an old tradition among engineers that the Trekkers among us may recall from the original show when the captain would pipe down to the engine room to ask how long it would take to repair damage and the chief engineer, Scotty, would estimate eight hours, only to be told "You've got two!" and somehow he always managed to meet these impossible goals.

As a child, I thought this was a testament to necessity being the mother of invention and heroic leadership, but in retrospect, I came to understand that Scotty was padding his estimates.

A DAY IN THE LIFE OF AN AGENCY PM

Ana Giraldo-Wingler, product manager at Coforma (coforma.io)

I check Slack when I wake up. I come to my computer 15 to 30 minutes before my first stand-up and create a note for the day in the Notes app before I start work, as soon as I sit down. I go to my note from the previous day and copy over all the items that are still not done yet, and I put it into my next day.

We do work for clients, which is different from being a PM at a start-up. The particular client that we're working with is the government, and the product that I'm working on is a replacement of a 20-year-old piece of software. So our requirements in a sense are different. It's not like we're building something that's never existed.

How each day is going to go really does depend on where we are within that sprint cycle. The first thing I think is "which Agile ceremonies either just occurred or are coming up?" If I know we have our sprint review coming up in two days on a Friday, my Wednesday is going to involve prepping the deck that I'm using to introduce the sprint review. I'm prepping the board to make sure that all the tickets are up-to-date and in the right list, etc.

As the PM, I have to facilitate communication between the engineering, design, and business layers so that things are moving in a smooth fashion.

So the first Wednesday of the two-week sprint, we have a UX stand-up with myself, the UX designer, and our researcher, which is scheduled for 15 minutes, but ends up usually being 30.

Then we have our actual stand-up, which is 30 minutes after the UX check-in—both of which occur daily. That's the whole team, including the developers, and we also have a project lead, which is interesting. I've never worked as a PM on a project where there was a lead as well as a PM. That's a symptom of being part of an agency where she's in charge of the contract and our relationship with the main client. It allows me to focus on the product things rather than on client management.

The next thing that I have is a meeting about delivery scenarios and data-base access with our tech lead because we are currently working with the government trying to get access to their infrastructure. It's taking longer than we anticipated, so we don't have the access that we need in order to build what we need to build. So that means we need to do a change of contract modification.

There's a break I have here from 11:00 a.m. to noon, and sometimes I will have to take my lunch early due to the East coast correlation.

Then we have a meeting with stakeholders within the government to talk about some open design/product questions that we had with them. We've tested them with users. We've gotten some feedback, and now we have some questions for the stakeholders to get their input on our iteration.

Then we have another meeting with different stakeholders called a *co-design* session with them, which is really fun because these guys are so creative and excited, and they've been using the current product for so long. They've been accumulating all these ideas for how to improve it. One of them actually built the original product in the nineties, and the other one has been using the product. So the co-creation is with people who are deeply knowledgeable about it. We literally have Figma open, and we have our designs, and we're dragging things around. That's cool.

We also have to coordinate with a different organization that's building the API that we're building our app on top of, to make sure they're giving us the data that we need in the format that we need it in. Attending their working sessions with their stakeholders keeps us abreast of what they're doing. I'll usually pop into those and just listen for anything that might sound concerning, or that might not have been on my radar.

At this point, it's afternoon, like 4:00 p.m., and I have time to look at my Notes file for the day again to see what I still need to do. Sometimes your calendar's a brick wall, but also you have tickets to write and you have questions to answer. It's like meetings are work, but there's also other work. It's tempting to try to work during some meetings, which isn't great, but sometimes that needs to happen. ■

Key Insights

- Engineers, like designers, are makers, and managers, including PMs, should be thoughtful about when and how to interrupt their creative flow.

- Product managers engage with their developers in a series of check-in cycles of increasing timescale called *cadences*.

- Day-to-day tactical PM work revolves around sprints that tend to last two to four weeks.

- Working with engineers effectively depends on cultivating mutual respect, both by showing interest and fluency with technical concepts and programmer folkways and by engaging intelligently in clarifying discussions about technical matters while gaining mastery of the technical architecture and landscape.

- A product manager has to learn how to negotiate and collaborate with engineers by being very attentive to their drives, concerns, and patterns of behavior.

CHAPTER 5

The Business of Product Is Business

For many designers, *business* is a dirty word. It conjures up images of "suits" who don't care about users—er, humans…no, people—the way you do, of bean counters, and of overseers cracking the whip and driving "death marches" to hit arbitrary dates and ship the requisite number of lines of code.

This isn't fair, of course, and not only does it represent a barrier to overcome if you want to go down the product management career path, but any such aversion to the business side of software development can hamper your UX growth and development as well.

Build Sustainable Value

As you know by now, the role of a product manager is to build value. This goal deliberately leaves unstated to whom that value accrues. As a user experience expert, naturally you will think in terms of valuable experiences for your customers who are deriving value from using your product.

The business, the organization that is building and delivering this software, also needs to reap some of the value being generated, in order to sustain itself and live. Paying attention to that side of the equation doesn't make you greedy or uncaring, and going out of business because you can't figure out how to make a living selling your valuable wares will equally deprive your customers of the virtues of what you're making.

Getting the balance right means neither raking too much value off the top so that the quality suffers, nor leaving too much value on the table so that the business fails to sustain itself.

So what is unsustainable value? Offering your services at a loss to corner a market is unsustainable. Building a business that can only scale by adding more staff is unsustainable. Making a profit by externalizing the costs of your business and in the process destroying the infrastructure and environment necessary for the operation of the market is also not sustainable.

Thinking in Terms of the Market

Sometimes you hear a word so often that you don't stop to think about what it means. *Market* can mean several things—from the place where people buy and sell (such as a farmers' market or supermarket) to the more abstract markets where securities are exchanged. In the context of this book, the word *market* really just means "a specific category of potential buyers."

Both UX and product management share roots in 20th century marketing business practices. In many ways, user experience is just a newer model of understanding and addressing the needs of customers, which has always been the primary goal of marketing efforts. Also, product management derives some of its DNA from product marketing (and still collaborates or overlaps with marketing departments around the product marketing concept in many organizations).

Product management goals often revolve around three stages of engagement with a product market:

- Identify and target a juicy market.
- Deeply understand its problems and needs, and then design and develop a solution to that problem that "fits the market."
- Figure out a way to bring the solution to the target market.

Targeting a Market

The earliest stage of the product life cycle focuses on identifying a suitable market to "go after" in the first place. This needs to be one that has a real problem you can solve, and it also needs to be a big enough market to justify investing a lot of time and energy and taking on the risk of a new venture.

Sizing a Market

When you are trying to determine what market to go after, or if a particular market is large or needy enough to sustain your line of business, it's tempting to cast the net as wide as possible. Who is this product for? Everybody on the planet! Adults age 24 to 65. Right-handed people! But the problem then becomes "How do you target such a vaguely defined heterogeneous group?" If you're not selling fizzy sugar water, how do you leap directly to mass appeal?

Now if your target market is "adults in the United States aged 18–35 who are thinking about buying their first new car," you've got some definition there to work with and a much better chance of crafting experiences and narratives that reach this market.

Once you have a handle on the types of people you are trying to serve, you can do some basic Google-type research to get a rough idea of the size of that market overall. Then you'll need to come up with and justify the percentage of that market that you think you can reasonably obtain as customers.

DO YOUR OWN RESEARCH

> Matt LeMay says, "Honestly, 90% of 'research' for product managers is just 'Googling stuff.'"

Here is where numeracy really helps. It's amazing how often people reason something like this about markets: "Well, there are a hundred million people in my target market, so I only need to reach 10% of them to have ten million customers!" or even "... I only need to reach 1% of them to have a million customers!" and sure, 10% is only a small part of the whole and jeez 1% is tiny! However, the ease of capturing "a mere 1%" is an illusion that is based on a huge denominator (Figure 5.1).

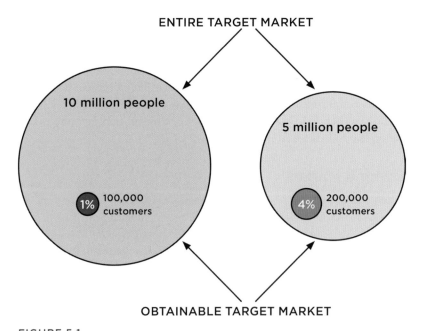

ENTIRE TARGET MARKET

10 million people

1% 100,000 customers

5 million people

4% 200,000 customers

OBTAINABLE TARGET MARKET

FIGURE 5.1
Reaching 100,000 customers out of a target market of 10,000,000 vs. 200,000 customers out of a better-defined target market of 5,000,000 isn't easier just because 1% sounds smaller than 4%.

It's not significantly easier (or even necessarily easier at all) to reach a million customers out of a target market of a hundred million than it is to reach a million customers out of a target market of four million. It definitely affects how and where you target your messaging and how you understand the needs of the market segment you are going after, but having a rough idea of the size of the potential market is really just the first step.

Gauging Interest

After you've identified your target market, it's time to better understand what the people in that market are crying out for and whether what you are offering (or planning to make for them) is even something they would need.

FROM THE TRENCHES...

WHERE THERE'S SMOKE...

One product I worked on, CloudOn, was a document editor for iPads before Word or Google Docs were available there. Jay Zaveri, chief product officer (and my boss and mentor at CloudOn), established that there was a market demand for "Word on the iPad" in the face of skepticism that anybody would want to do "real work" on a tablet.

The way he made the case to the rest of the leadership team and the company's board was by taking out a relatively cheap Google AdWords buy that said something along the lines of "Word is coming to the iPad! Sign up to be notified when it's here." (This is sometimes called a *smokescreen* test.)

He quickly gathered thousands and then tens of thousands of email addresses from people who were eager to do productive work on their convenient portable touch-screen devices. Not only did the upsurge in interest help justify the R&D direction that eventually led to a native gesture-based document editor for tablets (and a collaborative model for working with cloud documents that lives on today after CloudOn's sale to Dropbox), but it also helped with the initial go-to-market plan.

There are many ways to gauge interest in and validate an idea. Some are more qualitative—to the point of being anecdotal or potentially limited to confirmation bias—that is, if you only investigate like-minded people. Other methods are more qualitative and evidence based.

Finding Product-Market Fit

The next product phase addressing "markets" is the ubiquitous search for *product-market fit*. Despite the mystique this phrase has accrued (What is it? How do you know when you have it?), there's nothing tricky about these words. It literally just means that the product fits the needs of the market in some demonstrable way. But the phrase is also used to describe a stage in the life of a product or a product company.

Before achieving product-market fit, a product is still in search of a sustainable relationship with its customers. At this stage, it makes no sense to optimize things or to invest in heavily engineered aspects of the solution because you really don't know yet how badly people want what you're offering. The whole job right now is to find that product-market fit by paying close attention to what initial customers and their behaviors are telling you, by understanding as effectively as you can why noncustomers are staying away or failing to convert, and by experimenting relentlessly until things click.

Searching for product-market fit is a huge part of early-stage PM work, such as angel-funded start-ups and enterprises opening new lines of business or launching entirely new products in existing lines. For other PMs, product-market fit is a done deal, and the job has more to do with optimizing functionality, growing the market, upselling, and so on.

Now, to be totally honest, as with so many other rubrics, the concept of product-market fit is both subjective and somewhat arbitrary.

Like the stone in the "stone soup" parable, it provides an anchoring concept that enables good things to happen, but don't treat it like an objective yes/no fact. Even if you're measuring a quantity as a proxy for it, treat it like a qualitative thing.

"If They'll Crawl Through Glass..."

The holy grail for some entrepreneurial-minded product folks is a company that has achieved product-market fit with a lousy product. How is that possible? Well, if people want something badly enough, they will crawl through glass to get it. This does not mean that lining your entranceway with broken glass is a great user experience. It means that what you are offering meets people's needs to such an extent that they will put up with a subpar experience to get it.

This kind of scenario is a gold mine because it suggests that simply by improving the product experience in fairly straightforward ways, you will be able to capitalize on the inherent value and appeal of the product experience and service being offered, reduce bounce and churn, help more people understand and engage with the product, and ultimately reach much greater markets beyond the early adopters willing to put up with all those cuts.

7 CUPS

A big reason why I took on the head of product role at 7 Cups, a mental health community, was that just a little over a year since its founding as a YCombinator start-up, it was demonstrating that "crawl through glass" level of product-market fit.

The entire service was built by one engineer using ready-made web technologies and services, and it had grown in a sprawling organic way by responding to feedback from early adopters, so as a product, it left a lot to be desired. It was unfocused. It wasn't clear how to get started. It offered too many options that seemed similar to each other and too many navigation choices. Nevertheless, it was growing at a rapid clip.

Whatever 7 Cups had to offer (which was on-demand support from real people, with minimal waiting) was compelling and desirable enough that people were willing to put up with a lot of subpar "plumbing" and product experience to get it. What a ripe opportunity!

Zeroing In on Product-Market Fit

One of the most effective methods for quantifying product-market fit is to survey existing users and ask them how they would feel if the product went away. Would they be very disappointed, somewhat disappointed, or not disappointed at all?

This is subjective, of course, but there is a broad consensus among investors and product folk that if around 40% of your users would be "very disappointed" to lose your product, then you have product-market fit.

So, there are ways to determine whether you have this fit, but what if you don't? If the lack of fit comes from not enough customers who would miss your product if it went away, then the solution is to find and focus more on those customers who are already in your dedicated group (the ones who would be "very disappointed" to lose you).

Can you find more of these people and stop going after the rest? Can you convert more of your customers into feeling the way these people do? Anything you might want to try will come down to understanding these different subgroups better and learning what distinguishes them. What are the unique characteristics of the people in your market who are clamoring for your product?

Rahul Vohra, the founder and CEO of an email product called *Superhuman* shared a pretty good tactical process for achieving product-market fit with a customer base that was not there yet, which he called the *product/market fit engine*. He recommended that after surveying customers in the way just described, that you also ask the people who loved your product (the ones who would be very disappointed without it) what exactly they loved about it.

Then you segment your users (the market segments will depend on you, but one example he gave was segmenting people by job title) and analyze which segments are heavily represented in your strong group.

This process enables you to notice which segments or demographics to focus on (the ones most strongly represented among those who love your product) and which to consciously neglect (the ones who wouldn't mind if it went away). Then by analyzing what people love about your product, you can both double down on these things as you retarget the people, such as your best customers, and also start to figure out which demographics would be somewhat disappointed but could be converted to the "very" group if you offered them things they would love as well (Figure 5.2).

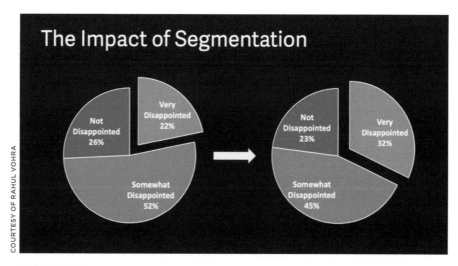

COURTESY OF RAHUL VOHRA

FIGURE 5.2

Rahul Vohra's "product/market fit engine" helps demystify the process of focusing on the customers most likely to love you back. He explains the whole process in an article called "How Superhuman Built an Engine to Find Product/Market Fit."

What Is the Go-to-Market Plan?

If you've identified a market need and believe you've got a solution that fits the problem, you still need to know how to get your product into the hands of the customers in your target market. Start-ups may launch first and iterate toward fit, but a mature company that takes marketing seriously needs to coordinate launches with growth strategies and messaging.

You'll hear "go-to-market" used as an adjective describing a type of strategy or plan, also often called a *launch plan*. Although a product can go through many launches (new versions, key features, and so on), go-to-market typically refers to the initial launch of a new product and its first encounter with the market that it was theoretically defined to satisfy.

A go-to-market strategy is a comprehensive plan that has the following features:

- Promotes awareness of your product in your target market
- Enables people to discover what your product has to offer
- Communicates a narrative in which the potential customer is the hero and their heroic journey involves embracing your product
- Lines up and coordinates with partners and other business-development stakeholders
- Produces marketing and potential advertising materials
- Sets the pricing model for the product
- Addresses the personnel and budgetary resources required to successfully launch the product to its market

Going to market generally involves coordinating with other stakeholder groups in your organization outside of the product team—most notably marketing, business development, sales, customer success, and customer support, but others may be involved as well.

NOTE A ROADMAP VS. A LAUNCH PLAN

Remember that a launch plan is *not* a product roadmap, but often when stakeholders ask for the roadmap, they are really asking for commitments about when features are going to ship. More on this later, in Chapter 10, "Roadmaps and How to Say 'No'."

Go-to-market has also come to be used at times as a noun describing all of the related activities involved in a go-to-market strategy.

In the case of CloudOn, when it came time to ship version 1 (which was initially called App2You, believe it or not) of the iPad app to the App Store, Jay was able to send a promotional email message to the tens of thousands of eager potential customers who had asked to be notified when it was available.

This email drove a downloading frenzy that had several immediate effects:

- CloudOn hit number one in Apple's productivity apps charts the day of launch.
- CloudOn hit the top ten list for all apps the day of launch.

- The prominent ranking in the charts drove much additional organic downloads beyond the initial group from the mailing list.
- This kept CloudOn high on both charts for several weeks as the initial surge gradually wore off.
- CloudOn had to limit downloads the first day because the server infrastructure was overtaxed by the unexpected enthusiasm.

Jay's initial "bet" that people wanted to work on their iPads was proven to be correct.

As a product manager, you may be involved with or be required to develop go-to-market strategies, or you may work on products that are well established and no longer manage incremental updates and changes in such an elaborate orchestrated way. Nevertheless, you should always try to understand and gauge the needs and frustrations of your target market, and every time you experiment with something new in your product, you need to bear in mind how you are going to deliver it.

Customer Obsession

Targeting the right customers and optimizing for their love requires the sort of deep study of users that is the bread and butter for a UX practitioner. The same fascination with users and proficiencies you have cultivated to understand their wants and needs will stand you in great stead in product management. A big part of the PM's job is to obsess about customers and to talk to them as frequently as possible.

As a PM, you'll jump at the chance for any new information about customers—new survey responses, updated traffic and behavior data, complaints on social media, reviews on the app store, direct feedback on existing or proposed designs, and more.

The best product organizations will foster strong ties between the product team and customer support, customer success, and community managers who have their fingers directly on the pulse of the user base. These people should be your new best friends. Often, they are frustrated by not having a direct conduit to the product team, and have insights and observations to share that are solid gold for your understanding.

You can do this in two ways:

- Set up formal processes for syncing, coordinating, and reviewing data and plans together.
- Alongside the formal cadences of checking in, build up more informal, back-channel relationships characterized by mutual support and collaboration.

Launching vs. Optimizing

In some sense, most product managers are always launching something. It may not be the debut of an entirely new category-defining product, but in any given sprint, you might be launching the 4.3 version of your mobile app, or your new search feature, or an AI chatbot, or something on a fairly regular basis. The exceptions to this tend to occur inside huge enterprises with 18-month-long waterfall software development lifecycle (SDLC) processes, or a no-longer-innovative business that forever finds excuses to hold off on shipping anything to avoid rocking the boat.

However, it's also a generally accepted notion among product leaders that some product managers are better at launching new things, while others are better at optimizing things that are already up and running. Again, this does not mean you have to have one type of PM to *launch* your product and then immediately bring in another type to *maintain and optimize it*. But on the level of any given product line, product, feature, or functionality, getting the thing to exist at all deals with one set of factors. Bringing out the best in it involves another.

It's a good idea to get a sense of where you think you fall on this spectrum. Do you relish the exhilaration of launching things into the unknown? Are you a skydiver at heart? Do you draw energy from seeing things turn from ideas into reality? Then you're probably something of an instigator, and your energy fits well with innovation and novelty.

Or do you prefer shaping and molding and guiding a team or initiative to its highest level of performance and success? Are you the sort of person who would rather join the crew of a well-designed, built, and maintained ship and "find out what it can really do!"? If so, then you might be more suited to taking on an existing product and improving it systematically, finding breakthrough opportunities, growing engagement and profitability, or even evolving it into a platform.

Maybe both of these things sound great to you, so a tight team where individual PMs are given wide latitude might suit you best.

These aren't mutually exclusive tendencies by any means. Hà Phan, a product leader and general manager at Pluralsight, and one of my product mentors, put it this way:

> For a long time I saw myself as the person who always starts things but never optimizes. Then when I started building this team, what evolved over time is I realized that I'm building a *platform*, building a *system*. So the system is a long game. You can't go "short game."

> So that's actually how I see it now: I'm doing both. I'm always starting new things and I'm always optimizing old things (or less new things).

Business Operations

Most of the time, if people ask you about your business skills as a product manager, if they're not asking about how you go to market, then they are thinking of finance or operations and general management.

You've probably picked up on the fact that product management has a large operational component, drawing both from *project* management (at the tactical product owner/scrum master interface) and from *program* management (in the coordination of people, teams and resources to achieve complex ambitious goals).

Some people became UX designers because they like to draw and are happiest when someone else is watching the deadlines and cracking the whip. If that's you, then product management is likely to feel like all the boring parts of school to you, with no recess.

But if you're the sort of UX designer who loves facilitating workshops and jumps up to the whiteboard to help facilitate a discussion by helping your colleagues articulate their concerns, or if you've tasted the operational and people management aspects of being a design manager and found them to your liking, then you'll likely take to that "business" aspect of product management readily.

It's worth noting that all disciplines tend toward people and program management as you rise through the ranks, so in that sense, this is less about product managers being business heads and more about management and organizational leadership in general.

Nonetheless, to be taken seriously as a product manager, you will need to demonstrate that you can be organized, keep complicated projects with multiple moving parts aligned and on track, and have the communication and people skills needed to motivate and support teams of people as they strive to work together in complex environments.

UX SUPERPOWER ALERT
STAKEHOLDERS ARE USERS TOO

A huge aspect of getting things done operationally is stakeholder management. This is another time when interpersonal skills and an ability to understand people come in handy. Start-up founder and user experience, research, and product management consultant Noreen Whysel observed: "Your skills that you develop as a UX designer help you to understand the business needs, because you can use the same techniques on the business side, on the stakeholder side, to find out what is it that they need because in a way, they're a 'user' too."

Financial Business Skills

When it comes to finance, though, it's likely you are treading in an area that never really came up doing UX research, strategy, or design. Because most of the team does not report to a product manager, PMs rarely have profit and loss (P&L) ownership over the product they work on, but even so, it behooves a PM to understand what the team is costing the business and what monetary value it is delivering.

Not only does this directly bear on how well the team is performing, but it also gives the PM a heads up if their business unit is a cost center and potentially vulnerable to the winds of change.

Not all product roles deal with transactions or revenue, but doing the job always requires a certain degree of savvy about how the money flows through the business and in and out of the product and the team building it. Making the case for a strategic priority is always on some level a competition for scarce resources.

As a product manager, your responsibility for cultivating and developing *value* applies every bit as much to the need to generate literal financial value to the business (or organization) underwriting the code you're developing and shipping, as it accrues to the customer or end user you're serving.

For the most part, financial concerns enter the picture in terms of pricing of product and features, revenue models, and the search for profitability. More on that in Chapter 8, "Getting the Money."

Business-to-Business (B2B) Products

Perhaps the product management space that is most steeped in business thinking and business contexts is B2B (business to business, as opposed to B2C for business to consumer, B2G for business to government, and B2B2C for business to business to consumer), meaning businesses whose customers are other businesses. There's a lot of money to be made selling tools and services that businesses need to make their own money. Some have compared this to the Levi Strauss strategy of getting rich selling canvas and tent stakes to gold miners instead of going out to pan for gold directly.

In a B2B context, concepts such as markets and customers shift to become both smaller and less abstract. Sales are made to businesses, not to individuals. The end user is often not the payer (the "customer"), which means that delighting the user will not directly influence their willingness or ability to pay. Also, customers are specific people at specific businesses known to your sales and account management colleagues, not the general public or everyone who can find a Google window, which affects many of your strategies in terms of understanding user behavior, talking to users and customers, and even trying to do statistically valid data analyses (something you'll hear more about in Chapter 6, "Product Analytics: Growth, Engagement, Retention").

To give a feel for how the role varies when your customers are businesses and not consumers, here is another day in the life of a product manager, in this case from Clement Kao, a product manager at Blend, which makes software for banks. (He is also the author of *Breaking into Product Management* and host of one of the best product management communities of practice online, Product Manager HQ).

A DAY IN THE LIFE OF AN ENTERPRISE PM

Clement Kao, a product manager at Blend

I wake up around seven. While I'm eating breakfast, I look through Slack and email, just trying to get a pulse of the things I need to be aware about today while I take the time to have a nice slow breakfast before it becomes super hectic. The first 10 minutes of my "workday" are spent checking all the calendar events that I have, trying to understand what my one priority is for today.

One of the challenges in B2B is that you don't get easy access to your users because you're gated through the account. Typically, in B2C, you can recruit users easily for user testing. It's relatively straightforward to be able to get people to look at your stuff.

In our business, we need to make sure that we are empowering our account managers to continue to deepen the relationship rather than have it be super "thrashy." So there's typically some amount of lead time needed to figure out how we want to position this. When is the right time to bring it up?

For example, in the morning, I might be working with three to four different account managers—all trying to work through what the objective is of this ask that we're making to their customers and users.

One nice thing about having these deeper relationships with these accounts is that they bring their end-users' qualitative feedback to you and say, "There's a problem. We're escalating it." Whereas in B to C, if your user doesn't like your product, they leave.

To wrap up the meetings with account managers, it's really important to determine *who, what, and when*. Like, "We agreed you all are writing emails. When will you send them out? And if they haven't responded back by what time frame, when are you going to follow up with them? Let's make sure that we're really clear as to how we are prioritizing this. What are the next steps?"

Now it's lunch time. This is during the pandemic, and I want to make sure that I have time to myself to reset. I'm going to step away from the computer and make lunch with my significant other. Cooking lunch typically takes 30 to 40 minutes, and then we'll eat for 15, and then I'll walk around a little bit, get back to my desk, and then jump right back in.

For the afternoon, I turn to a different feature that I own, which I am trying to bring to the finish line.

I think one of the things that we have to keep in mind in B2B is that people are using not just your feature, but also your entire product to run their business. There are all of these other features that are floating out there, so you can't just optimize for your own retention, engagement, and usage because if you just optimize for yourself, you're going to break other people's workflows.

Whatever we design and build, when we deliver it to a customer, they don't just accept it. It's not like Facebook messenger. It's not like Instagram, where users might complain, but then they get used to it. There's no doing that in B2B because they have all these employees who are trained on all of these scripts on all of these rollout plans.

As the product manager working directly with a lot of these pilot customers, my role is to provide more of the lens of not just what the user will say, but what a customer executive might say when we propose this direction or scope or change management.

Next, I'm going to sit down with my product operations team to understand how the rollout of a past feature has been working. How do we see the adoption for different customers? We might draw on data, in terms of usage, or we might draw on qualitative account management feedback, like "We are hearing that this account is really struggling with this," and basically working with product operations to understand for a feature that is in flight how we should fine-tune the messaging to make sure that our customers can adopt it.

Because again, I don't just ship it and then watch the data flow in. I need to train all my internal stakeholders first. "This is what this does. This is how it works. And don't turn these other things on because they're currently in progress. And if you turn them on, then stuff will break."

So we are in the late afternoon now, and there is some customer reporting that there is an urgent thing that is broken. They're freaking out about it, and they need someone to take a look. So what I do first is jump in to understand it.

Do we have enough information from the customer to actually know what we are supposed to do from an engineering perspective? What is the breadth of impact? Who is being impacted? If I staff engineers against it too early, they're going to say I don't have enough information.

We spin up a zoom "war room," and we start working through the triage together until we figure it out and have a fix. When we know how we're going to hot fix it, we'll figure out the release plan.

This is a long day because there's a production fire. I need to go loop in legal compliance, and infosec (information security) on my side, to make sure that we understand the impacts of the bug and the fix, because sometimes the fix might actually cause even more problems.

Then we assemble our internal communication. While engineering is still working through how we're going to release the fix, it's my job to figure out how we are going to release the communications.

Once we've got the communications out, we're all good. The fire has died.

At this point, I usually look back on the day before I step away, and ask "Did I do the thing that I said I wanted to get done today, early in the morning?" If not, I think about how this affects my initiatives for the rest of this week. Are there things that I now need to reorder based on what has happened today? That way, I can understand what my future workflow is going to look like.

My day ends there. I make dinner and spend the rest of the night not looking at Slack. ∎

Key Insights

- Business is not a dirty word.
- Product is responsible for building value both for customers and for the organization, so that it may sustain itself.
- Product management demands deep understanding of a target market and a solid strategy for how to capture a percentage of it.
- For a new product, achieving "product-market fit" is job one and until you have it, time spent adding features or polishing bugs is wasted.
- Great product managers are obsessed with their customers (both past, present, and future) and ravenous for any morsel of insight into them.
- Some product managers are better at launching products and others are better at bringing out the best in existing products.
- People and program management are a huge part of your product and get to be even more important as you rise to leadership.
- Business also means money.
- For some products, your customer is another business.

CHAPTER 6

Product Analytics: Growth, Engagement, Retention

O f all the things that product managers do that UX people tend *not* to do, data analysis is perhaps the most alien to the design world. Even the business aspects of product management that give some designers the heebie jeebies can still be framed and understood in familiar terms: solving problems, designing solutions that address competing needs, and so on. It's also true that many savvy UX researchers, strategists, and designers do consume data intelligently, use it wisely to inform their processes, and recognize the value of combining quantitative insights with qualitative ones.

But... almost uniformly, even among the UX practitioners who embrace data analysis fully as a tool of their trade, there is very little appetite for spending a majority of their time staring at columns of numbers, data tables, or analytical models (let alone building, testing, and deploying analytical models). Very few people got into design or UX out of a love of number crunching. Not saying it's not possible, but it's vanishingly rare.

It's no exaggeration to say that product managers may spend a majority of their time analyzing data. There are definitely roles and even periods of time in most product roles when understanding the data is almost a full-time job. For a certain kind of geek, this is actually super fun.

Living in the Data

I call this "living in the data." You might call it "swimming in the data"—diving deeply and exploring widely. This daily practice of immersing yourself in your data leads eventually to something like a feel for the data, for its grain, its granularity, its cycles, and other "little ways," in an almost ambient sense.

FROM THE TRENCHES...

THE REALITY BEHIND THE DATA

Matt LeMay, co-founder and partner of Sudden Compass, has a more humanistic way of describing this same sort of immersion: "I call it 'living in your user's reality.' It's important to remember that data is a proxy for other things—I've seen a lot of product managers spend forever on dashboards but never actually learn directly from their customers."

An obsessed product person will wake up wondering what the daily metrics look like, will peek at a North Star metric frequently, will set up alerts to notice when key data points suddenly jump to values far outside of the usual parameters, will not be satisfied passively consuming a so-called dashboard, and will instead be engaged constantly in an interactive practice of interrogating, massaging, pivoting, and slicing the data to tease out meaning wherever possible.

Or, at the very least, to tease out some clues, some hints worth researching qualitatively to go from a curious "what" to a satisfying explanatory "why" and from that to an actionable "how."

Get to Love SQL

A common concern for folks getting into software product management, especially those with humanities degrees or art skills, is "how technical do I have to be?" As discussed in Chapter 4, "Wrangling Engineers," it depends on the role, but generally it has more to do with conversancy with technical concepts and constraints than with being able to craft production-ready code yourself or single-handedly design the architecture of a technical system.

But one technical skill that all product managers should embrace is the ability to query databases and manipulate data. If you're fortunate, you'll work with product analytics software that produces charts and results and even some analyses at the press of a button, but there are times when there is no substitute for "getting under the hood" yourself to interact with and sift through the data directly.

You may even want to take a class in MySQL or any other SQL (Structured Query Language) flavor to learn the basics of command-line database querying. This knowledge empowers you to ask your own questions of the data without having to ask an engineer to pull up a data set or for a data analyst to set up a special view for you in an app such as Tableau.

Or at Least Airtable...

With the onset of tools such as Airtable that make database creation, import, manipulation, and querying much easier by providing a complete tabbed spreadsheet-type user interface, you may find you can get by without typing any SQL code at all into a command-line. However, even low-code or no-code solutions such as this will only take you so far, so it empowers you, as a product manager, to be able to fend for yourself when it comes to data.

Make Instrumentation Part of Every Feature

A common learning cycle for PMs is to ship a product, feature, or fix and then realize afterward that it needs "instrumentation" (product hooks added to the code to capture user and system-driven events for analysis), so you make sure that will be done in the next sprint, but meanwhile you are flying blind for the first few weeks of your new product.

So then you get serious about instrumentation and add it to your spec template as an item to address. At this point, you should connect it back to the goals you are trying to accomplish with this project and figure out how to measure success. Then you can work with your developers to include this instrumentation with the feature at launch, which is a huge victory.

After this, you tend to realize you are still doing this ad hoc with each new spec and that you need to work with your engineering peers to define conventions or adopt a system that enables instrumentation to be applied to any event and to follow naming conventions defined in a taxonomy somewhere.

Eventually, it becomes second nature that you never build and ship anything without fully instrumenting it in a way that is consistent with the rest of your product.

UX SUPERPOWER ALERT
FINDING OUT WHY

With your background in user experience, you are uniquely positioned to drive conversations from the "what" found in the data to the "why" that you can only really discover through qualitative research. If you have fully embraced the need for data, you are also that much more credible when you explain the need to close the loop and investigate the signals by talking to people.

Funnel Optimization

One of the most common ways to study data and gain insights into how to make parts of your product work together is called *funnel optimization*. The funnel metaphor is a strange one if you think about it. It's primarily visual, rather than logical. The idea is something like this: In most online processes (or really any sort of task a lot of people attempt), there are a sequence of steps, and it is rare for everyone who embarks on step one to make it all the way through to the final step in any process.

In fact, there tends to be a drop-off at every step along the way. This drop-off varies greatly, of course. Some steps are trivial or so pleasant that 100% of the people who complete the previous step complete the next one, but as a rough rule of thumb, you're likely to lose 10% right off the top every time you add another step to a process.

Why a Funnel?

OK, but why is it called a *funnel*? Well, imagine it as shown in Figure 6.1, with a bunch of people starting on the first step of a process and much fewer making it to the end.

Number of People to complete the step

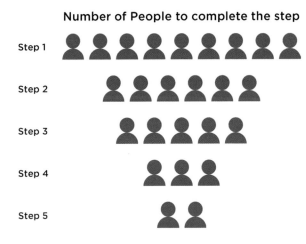

FIGURE 6.1
Imagine a five-step process where nine people complete step 1 and only two complete the final step. If you look at how many people were lost at each step along the way (and maybe also squint a little bit), you can see why people started calling this pattern a funnel.

So it got called a funnel because of the superficial visual resemblance to something wide at the top and narrow at the bottom. Never mind that a real funnel captures everything at the top and rushes it through the increasingly narrow hole at the bottom, which is definitely not what a "funnel" does.

How to Analyze a Funnel

There are several ways to look at a funnel to try to understand what is going on, why people drop off at various stages, and whether any of those patterns are changing over time or being affected by other factors.

One of the first things to do is to look for anomalous drop-offs at particular steps. Figure 6.2 shows the complete sign-up process for an online therapy service that involves a dialog with a chatbot, getting matched with a therapist, providing a credit card, and starting a free three-day trial.

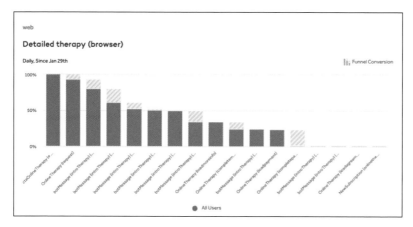

FIGURE 6.2

You can see that some people drop off at nearly every step in this funnel, but almost all drop off at one particular step.

In this chart, generated with Amplitude, the dark blue bars represent the percentage of people in a given time period who completed that step. The lighter blue striped parts show the portion that dropped off from the previous step.

You can see a bit of a drop-off at the first few steps, with a bigger drop-off heading into step 4 (just after the chatbot is introduced), and then a few more steps that carry nearly everyone along (they are easy-to-complete responses to chat questions).

Then there are a few steps where 1/4 to 1/3 of the people are lost. These steps bear closer scrutiny to find out what is happening here. Are the questions more challenging? Is the tone wrong? Is there something actually difficult or partly broken preventing some people from completing or understanding the step?

But there is one step that stands out in particular because the funnel loses nearly everyone at that point. Can you guess what the user is asked to do at that step? (If you guessed "reach into their wallet and pull out their credit card," you'd be right.)

Investigating Drop-Off

Now, bear in mind that the moment of truth is always going to show a larger-than-average drop-off. This is to be expected. Some people are just window-shopping. Many people do a final gut-check before committing to anything, let alone something that may cost money one time or even a recurring subscription.

Who among us has not abandoned an online shopping cart with something in it we decided at the last minute that we didn't really need? In fact, ecommerce shopping cart analysis is basically the origin of the kind of funnel analysis we are talking about, although it works equally well with nontransactional processes and tasks.

So, at this stage, it's time to investigate those steps that have unusually large drop-offs and come up with some hypotheses about what is causing the problem and how this cause might be addressed, mitigated, or worked around.

Can expectations be set better up front to avoid "sticker shock" when the price is revealed? Would quotations from happy customers persuade some reluctant free-trial sign-ups to complete the process? And so on.

Mind you, this is just one of the ways to investigate a funnel and the most obvious. Other questions to ask might include "Are all these steps really necessary?" meaning, would more people complete the process if you streamlined it a bit and removed some steps?

UX SUPERPOWER ALERT
SYSTEMS THINKING

The problem-solving techniques in the design toolkit can come in real handy when you're trying to explore ideas for why a funnel step is underperforming expectations, but be careful at the same time not to spend your entire focus on the problems that are most easily *solved* by design. Look to the whole system, the larger experience, the options being presented, the transactional considerations if any, and even data about the state of the world during the time you're studying, outside of your tiny product experience.

Monitoring Trends over Time

Another way to look at a funnel is from the side, meaning instead of focusing on the aggregated motion through the funnel in a given time period, to instead compare results across a time series. You can do this at the level of any of the steps (What percentage of people made it from step 3 to step 4 this week and how does that compare to the percentage who completed step 3 last week?), or across multiple steps, or even across the entire funnel (Which is the easiest way to see how a funnel is performing over time at a glance?).

Figure 6.3 shows the conversion rate of a funnel over twelve months. During this time, a series of experiments tested hypotheses about ways the funnel could perform better, and you can see gradual improvement over the course of the year: starting out nearly 1.2% of the people completed the funnel to approximately 1.7% later, something like a 40% improvement in the conversion rate.

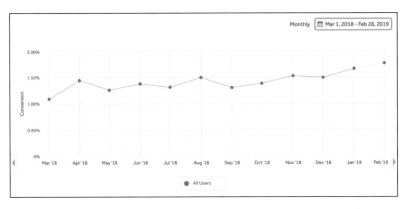

FIGURE 6.3
This funnel tracked conversion (completion of the final step) over time.

Abbreviated Funnels

For a multistep process, you can often get lost a bit in the weeds, so another way to look at your longer funnels is to instrument all the steps but then produce a chart that shows only the "major" steps or key milestones along the way. This approach can sometimes help declutter the chart and reveal the sections that need the most work, as opposed to the specific steps.

All of these ways of looking at the changing funnel data over time give you hints about where you can find improvement and how you can optimize the "throughput."

Funnel Caution

As with any form of experimentation, be careful that your focus on perfecting one particular funnel doesn't lead you to neglect other aspects of your product or even entirely different ways of designing the experience that might look quite different from your current funnel (different sequences, different interfaces or affordances, nonlinear pathways, and so on).

Optimizing a funnel can be a powerful, almost addictive, experience so don't let it blind you to the things going on in your product that are not as easily quantified or as well represented in the funnel you're working on.

Growth Metrics

When working with product analytics, nine times out of ten you are trying to find some way to make a key number bigger. Getting a data point to grow is about the most purely quantitative way you can view product work, and—as you may have encountered already in your own work—"growth" can be a specialty or even a department of its own, sometimes part of the product team and sometimes working at cross-purposes with it.

There are "growth hackers" out there who have made their careers through quasi-scientific experiments to rapidly or ferociously grow key metrics. These roles often combine product skills with programming chops. (The "hacker" part can refer either to this hands-on technical competence or to the larger notion of trying out ideas aggressively to find new ways to optimize growth that "hacks" the existing patterns.)

There are also product manager roles that are explicitly "growth product managers" tasked with this area of responsibility exclusively. But most product managers have a number somewhere they are assiduously working on to make grow.

The two most common growth targets are active user base and revenue. Almost always growing the user base comes first (you need people coming in the door before anyone is going to give you money).

Growing Your User Base like a Pirate

A few years back, an entrepreneur and investor from the eBay mob, Dave McClure, boiled down growth levers using the piratical mnemonic, AARRR (see Figure 6.4).

Customer Lifecycle: 5 Steps to Success

- **Acquisition**: users come to the site from various channels

- **Activation**: users enjoy 1st visit: "happy" user experience

- **Retention**: users come back, visit site multiple times

- **Referral**: users like product enough to refer others

- **Revenue**: users conduct some monetization behavior

AARRR!

Pirate

FIGURE 6.4
Dave McClure's handy mnemonic helps us remember some of the key levers of growth (in a start-up-oriented context).

As hard-core pirates, some pronounce this as AAARRR, including one further A at the top of this hierarchy:

- Awareness
- Acquisition
- Activation
- Retention
- Referral
- Revenue

You'll see that some versions of this mnemonic flip the last two items. Of course, revenue is not *always* the end goal in every growth effort, but it usually is for start-ups (the context from which this advice originated), and it does tend to be literally the bottom line in most forms of enterprise. (Even nonprofits or government bodies that don't typically use money transactionally still have budgets and expenses, for example.)

This sequence itself can be viewed as a sort of long-scale funnel, and instrumented as such as well. Each step along the way likely consists of multiple steps, so it can also be treated as a loose sequence of funnels.

Awareness

Awareness is the first step for any sort of user growth. Before people try your product, they need to know it exists. They have to have heard of it. Someone has to tell them about it, or they need to see an advertisement, or hear a marketing message, or find a link among their search results.

Awareness is about getting on the radar of your potential customers, and it overlaps with marketing (it basically is marketing) in the "product marketing" sweet spot. But, of course, awareness alone is not enough. Something needs to tip the person from knowing about your service to trying it.

Acquisition

Acquisition refers to turning a prospect into a user or customers, "acquiring" them for your user base. (The word feels a bit problematic, but it starts with A so there's that.)

Acquisition can be defined in various ways. Downloading your app from the store may count as acquisition. Visiting your website and interacting with the content may count as acquisition. One unequivocal form of acquisition is sign-up. If someone makes an account on your service, you may safely consider yourself to have acquired them.

It's easy to think of this as the key step. New customer acquired—achievement unlocked! But even a member sign-up is no guarantee of continued engagement, or that this user will become valuable to the success of the product, let alone revenue-generating. In order for that to happen, you need the person sampling your product to use it actively, to become what we call in the parlance, *an active user*.

Activation

A *user* is said to be "activated" or to have become "active" if they engage with the experience of a product in some meaningful way. A lot of product analytics software will default to referring to a user as active if they show up in the data at all. That is, imagine a user who downloads your app and tries it out on a Monday.

On Tuesday, they are busy and forget about it but something (maybe a push notification?) reminds them about it on Wednesday, and they log back in and poke around some more. Then on the weekend, they come back again on Saturday and Sunday.

This user will appear active on Monday, Wednesday, Saturday, and Sunday, but not on the other days of this week. They will also be counted as a weekly active user (one time) for the week these days appear in (or for two weeks if the time periods are cutting through the middle of this Monday–Sunday week), and for the month (or months) these days appear in.

> **NOTE** DAU, WAU, MAU
>
> Product folks tend to talk most about daily and monthly active users (I recall being pretty excited when a product I led hit a million monthly active users!), and sometimes weekly as well, all of which depend on the usage cadences of the product. These concepts get abbreviated to DAU (daily active users), WAU (weekly), and MAU (monthly), and one interesting analysis you can do is comparing them as a ratio, such as DAU/WAU or DAU/MAU (often expressed in terms of percentages). This can help show whether overall growth is flat, going up, or going down. So, for example, DAU/MAU tells you on average how many days of the month a typical user drops by. A 20% ratio means they were active for about six days in the month. As a rule of thumb, 40% is generally considered good, and anything above 50% is considered excellent, but this will actually vary depending on industry norms.

The problem with defining being active as "showing up" is that this overstates the case, counting folks who *churn* or *bounce* (leave the product or site again soon after arriving without having engaged in any meaningful way). So instead, it's more useful to require that a user exhibit some behavior. (Typically, you define a basket of events that qualify as making the user "active," and then identify all the users in a given time period who triggered any of the events in that basket.)

Another model is to track active users in the loose terms of anyone who showed up (it can make a nice "vanity metric" to impress friends and the less perspicacious investors), and to additionally track a separate metric called something like *engaged users* where the bar for counting as engaged instead of merely active is higher (requiring, for example, that they trigger an event from a smaller and more rigorous list).

You can then even compare your ratios of engaged users to active users to see where more lookie-loos can be converted to participants. Ultimately, the more engaged a person is with your product, the more likely you are to retain them in your user base.

Retention

Fundamentally, product growth relies on retention. Without robust retention, you can waste a lot of time, money, and energy building awareness, acquiring new users, and activating them, only to find that you've lost them in your leaky sieve, like trying to fill up a bucket with a hole in it.

Retaining a healthy percentage of the users who try your product is the one sure way to grow in a compounding way, so you will likely spend more time analyzing retention and looking for the combination of experiences that correlates best with a satisfied returning customer or member or client.

One quick way to study how well you are retaining users is by looking closely at new and returning users in any given time period. If the raw number of returning users (all users minus new users) is going up, that's a pretty good sign. If the percentage of returning users (all users minus new users, divided by all users) is going up, that's probably good (but it can also mean that your new-user acquisition isn't keeping up).

In the first chart in Figure 6.5, you can see a slight upward trend as returning monthly users head toward and eventually break 50k. The second chart shows that over that same time period the percentage of returning users grew appreciably from around 14% to around 18% (about a 30% increase).

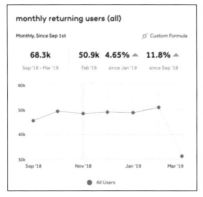

FIGURE 6.5

Monthly returning users for a product expressed first in absolute terms and then as a percentage.

The mainstay of retention analysis goes deeper than comparing raw totals of new and returning users and instead follows specific users in cohorts to track when and how often they come back after initially appearing.

Figure 6.6 shows a weekly retention analysis for nearly half a year. Week 0 is shown at 100%, which means that the people who were active in that week are the cohort we will be tracking and all of them were by definition active in that baseline week. Week 1 shows just upward of 25%, which means that a little over one in four of the people who came in the benchmark week returned a week later.

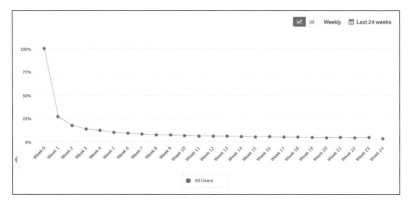

FIGURE 6.6

A weekly retention chart.

By week 2, we are closer to 20% and week over week fewer return in a familiar long-tail pattern that flattens out somewhere around 5% many weeks out. Now, this is not a funnel. There's nothing preventing the numbers for week 3 from being higher than those for week 2, for example, but the truth is that this rarely happens. Retention charts almost always look this way, but the goal is to get them higher.

NOTE **RETENTION**

> Retention can be calculated either in terms of the person returning on that specific day (which is the strict form) or the person having returned in any of the days up to and including that day (a looser calculation). Either analysis can show you interesting patterns.

Any one of the data points on a retention chart like the one in Figure 6.6 can also be compared to weeks (or days, or months) for other cohorts. So, for example, you might want to know that the cohort in Figure 6.6 had 10% retention in week 10. You could then run the same chart for people whose week 0 is one week later and see how their week 10 retention compares to 10%. This sort of time series analysis can also be plotted on a chart.

In Figure 6.7, the chart shows the change in monthly retention of signed-up members over time for mobile web users.

FIGURE 6.7

Member sign-up retention data for mobile web users.

Cohorts don't have to be strictly based on stretches of time. Cohorts are any groups of users collected for comparison purposes, so you can also query your data (depending on what you're collecting) to find left-handed users, users over the age of 50, users grouped by their language preferences, etc., and compare their retention over time to notice if there are lessons to be learned or advantages to be gained.

Referral

If you've reached the point in your growth efforts where you've optimized your awareness, acquisition, activation, and retention models, then driving up referrals is the next lever you can turn to, at least in some businesses. Remember that this "pirate" mnemonic is geared toward start-ups and not every model (such as, for example, most B2B businesses) is positioned to make use of referrals.

Once someone using your software has been activated, engaged, and retained, they probably like your product! They may even recommend it to friends. If you provide them with a way to do this (such as a share button), and build in triggers to suggest they recommend the app at moments when they are most likely to be inclined to do so, then you can start tracking which of your new users arrived by following a referral link from one of your existing customers.

Turning enthusiastic supporters into ambassadors or even evangelists for your product is the ultimate growth engine.

If you take the fraction of your users who recommend your product and then look at the percentage of those recommendations that deliver a new user, you can then calculate what is often called the *coefficient of virality*, and what it really measures is how many new customers you can obtain just on the back of your existing user base, without any additional marketing or advertising efforts to supplement.

Anyhow, here's the usual "virality" equation:

- No. of invitations sent out by each set of customers: i
- Percentage of invites converting into customers: c%
- So then the **viral coefficient (K) = i * c%**, and K is the number of customers each existing customer can convert successfully

If K is below 1, then your user base is going to shrink over time without additional acquisition. If it is 1, then you are at a break-even point, and so in theory any number above 1 is good and will help

MAYBE "VIRAL" ISN'T THE BEST METAPHOR?

Now, to be honest, in this day and age I really don't like the metaphor of the virus. Let's work on some healthier terminology, shall we? One person who has thought about this a lot is Kevin Marks, who wrote a blog post called "How Not to Be Viral" (over a decade ago) in which he recommended several potential alternative metaphors to embrace, all looking to nature but away from disease models (warning that anything that behaves like a disease is going to trigger an immune response):

Scattering lots of seeds (r-Strategy, used by many plants and animals)

Nurturing your young (k-Strategy, used by mammals)

Fruiting ("delicious with a seed in it")

Rhizomatic ("from the roots up")

Maybe you can come up with some more?

growth, although a K factor of 15 is obviously going to help a lot more than a factor of 1.02.

A nice thing about the referral model is that it closes the loops, and if you have a sufficiently high coefficient of spread, then you can start to get virtuous cycles driving all your growth numbers upward.

Revenue

The final R in the pirate mnemonic is about the money. For start-ups, it really is all about getting to sustainability, so revenue is frequently the key growth metric to optimize. Of course, early-stage start-ups often don't have any revenue, and in those cases, user growth is treated as a proxy for eventual potential revenue growth.

See Chapter 8, "Getting the Money," for more on revenue modeling and optimization.

Two Cautions

Data gets a bad rap in the UX world sometimes, as it can be associated with ignoring the humane aspects of a software experience in the service of making some specific numbers go up. But data analysis is just a tool in the toolkit alongside contextual inquiry and journey mapping, to name a few at random. It is neither inherently good nor evil, and its impact depends entirely on how it is utilized.

Having said that, there are two serious pitfalls to beware when obsessively trying to optimize important metrics:

- Resist the urge to optimize "dark metrics," meaning data powered by human unhappiness, deceit, or manipulation.
- Be very careful when choosing proxy metrics not to mistake the map for the territory.

These two dangers are of a somewhat different nature, as the first depends primarily on your values and your vigilance, and the second has to do more with reading too much into your own data.

Dark metrics are metrics that may benefit the business, particularly in the short term, but do so at the expense of tricking people (making it hard to cancel a subscription, let's say, or scraping their address book without permission or clear disclosure).

Bad proxy metrics can lead to you optimizing a number for its own sake, at the expense of the intended goal that the metric was chosen to represent.

There is a great example of this from the world of medicine. It's anecdotal, as I am not a doctor, so don't take my advice here, but the idea is this:

- High cholesterol is an indication of increased risk of heart attack.
- Taking statins can reduce one's cholesterol levels.
- But this reduction in the metric may not be correlated with any reduction in risk of a heart attack.

That is to say, it is possible to change the metric without improving the underlying situation that the metric was chosen to represent. So choose carefully and validate results with other indicators to avoid missing the forest for the trees.

Lukas Bergstrom, an ex-Google product consultant, made the point that at least some quantitative data needs to be regularly reality-checked with qualitative research: "At least I've found it helpful to think of the product metrics and qualitative deep dives as opposite poles that I need to always be moving between."

A DAY IN THE LIFE OF A GROWTH-STAGE PM

Janet Brunckhorst, director of product management, Aurora Solar, a "growth stage" (series B) start-up

Share anything else that might help describe the environment in which you practice product management.

Mix of R&D, established product, and new product for new segments.

How do you start your workday?

Before work, I write. This isn't for work per se, but it means I'm thinking about how teams are structured and how to make them better. I typically check Slack and email while I'm doing breakfast and getting kids ready so by the time I'm starting for real, I can focus on some work. If I don't have a meeting first thing, that will usually mean following up on questions from engineering, testing something, or some other tactical work.

How do you spend the early morning?

I'd love to say I spend my most productive hours digging into strategic work, but usually there's at least one meeting. If I can, I dive into a deeper topic.

How do you spend most of the morning?

Meetings.

How does the morning end?

Meetings. Twice a week I go to the gym at noon. I block out my lunch.

When do you take a lunch break?

Noon is my lunch break.

What do you do first thing in the afternoon?

Meetings. If I don't have a meeting, I sit down after lunch to dig into research or write some definition for upcoming products. Or prep for my next recruiting interview.

How do you handle "fire drills" or other unplanned work?

First, I try to get a clear sense of the urgency and reasons it's urgent. If it really is urgent, I give the relevant team a heads-up via Slack. If it's clear enough what needs to be done, we can generally sort that out on Slack and get started. If not, I will kick off a Slack conversation with the people who can clarify. Only if that doesn't work will I call a meeting. Sometimes, this means pushing back on an initial request to meet.

How do you spend the bulk of the afternoon?

Most days it's—you guessed it—meetings. Also testing anything that was completed, responding to requests and questions that came in during the morning. And hopefully, pushing the deeper work ahead. Some days we use the afternoon for workshops.

What do you do at the end of the workday?

Wrap up any last questions. Check my calendar for the following day. Shut down my computer.

Do you work in the evening?

When necessary. ■

Key Insights

- All great product managers spend time diving deeply into data and seeking to understand it as thoroughly as possible.

- You should learn to work directly with data to avoid dependence on others and to make data analysis an ordinary part of your day.

- Instrument (add product analytics to) everything you build, so that you won't be "flying blind" when you launch.

- Don't track everything: focus on key user and system events.

- Optimizing funnels can be a great complement to UX and other ways to improve an experience so that more people are able to complete it to their satisfaction.

- Not all product analytics boil down to growth, but many do.

- Growth actually consists of many different elements that can all contribute to a growing base of users, paying or otherwise. Among these are awareness, acquisition, activation (and engagement), retention, referral, and sometimes revenue (or AAARRR for short).

- Don't manipulate or harm people using the excuse that the data made you do it.

- Be careful not to chase the wrong metric off a cliff.

Testing Hypotheses with Experiments

Remember how a product manager needs to be a kind of scientist? Perhaps a mad scientist at times if you dream big—but always grounded in evidence, taking care to measure things accurately.

Scientists learn everything they can about a subject and wonder about the parts nobody seems to have a clear answer for yet. They develop hypotheses. This is the creative part! Hypotheses are ideas about why things are the way they are. Once you've got a hypothesis, you can work on coming up with ways to test it, to prove it true or disprove it. Whether the hypothesis is right or wrong, a good test will teach you something about what is going on.

UX SUPERPOWER ALERT
HYPOTHESES ARE JUST IDEAS TO EXPLORE

Generating hypotheses may sound like something you do in an ivory tower or laboratory, but it's just a fancy way of coming up with theories and ideas you can test out. Any design exploration you've ever done has been a way of testing hypotheses. User research scripts are based on hypotheses you want to explore. Don't let the science talk scare you. You've got this!

Experimentation as a Way of Life

A lot of product teams segregate experimentation from other software development activities (build and fix, primarily), either focusing a small team of engineers on experiments (possibly working with a growth-focused product manager or even a growth "hacker") or rotating experiments in on a cycle, such as every third sprint.

But this can be a reductive way to think about experimentation, almost always centered on the popular expedient of *bucket testing* (also called *split testing*, *A/B testing*, and *multivariate testing*).

The truth is that product management entails an endless series of "bets" that need to be tested and played out. Some are about launching something new and others about how to make things better (as discussed in Chapter 5, "The Business of Product Is Business"), but they all involve developing working hypotheses of what is going on, what is hindering progress, what would unlock better outcomes, and what to focus on next.

It is better to recognize that experimentation is a way of life and is threaded through all your decisions.

Build vs. Fix vs. Tune

One broad way to break down what a software development team can be working on at any given time is to note that the team is either building something new that does not yet exist, fixing bugs or other perceived deficiencies in some software that does already exist (but may or may not yet be released), or fine-tuning software that exists and has users and the potential to get better.

Experimentation plays a role in all of these phases of development:

- The determination about what to build, for what audiences, addressing which pain points they have in their current ways of doing what they do, and figuring out which "job" they will be willing to "hire" your software to do for them.

- Fixing bugs isn't particularly experimental, but prioritizing which bugs to fix (because bugs are kind of fractal-y, and you can't really ever fix them all for every scenario on every platform and device ever) represents a bet or testing of a hypothesis about what must work seamlessly for your customer and what will be good enough if it's good enough.

- Tuning for improved outcomes is almost entirely a matter of experimentation, and it's also the context in which most practitioners are highly aware of the experiments they are running.

Defining Hypotheses

A wise man once said "Hypotheses are ideas about why things are the way they are." Often, for a product manager, hypotheses are more specifically attempts to explain the perplexing or unpredictable results showing up in the data. You learned about product analytics, metrics, and data analysis in Chapter 6, "Product Analytics." Remember that a PM tends to be obsessed with certain key North Star metrics, frequently going so far as to arrange for a daily morning email or Slack update, and poring over standing reports and charts whenever time presents itself.

One reason you might look at the same key North Star metrics every morning is so that you notice when they go wonky. Why did sales drop to zero at midnight last night? Why are downloads 4x the usual number today? Why are you trending on Twitter?

PROBING FOR CLARITY AND UNDERSTANDING

When I worked at 7 Cups, our service relied on volunteers trained to provide active listening to people seeking free emotional support online. We called these volunteers our *Listeners*. At one point, we had a button on our global menu that read "Become a Listener," and we felt it could perform better as a recruiting affordance.

A conversational designer on my team, Heather Cornell, suggested the hypothesis that "New visitors to our website don't know what a Listener is, let alone why they should want to become one." This seemed pretty compelling, but how could we test it?

Cornell proposed we try a different label for the button, such as "Volunteer as a Listener" or "Become a Volunteer." Both of those alternatives performed better than "Become a Listener" did, and "Volunteer as a Listener" performed best of all. You can still see that option in the top menu at 7 Cups last time I checked (Figure 7.1).

FIGURE 7.1
7 Cups still has "Volunteer as a Listener" in its global navigation.

A hypothesis and experiment led us to the realization that there were a lot more people out there looking for volunteer opportunities than looking to take on a specific named role at one particular volunteer organization, as seen in the global navigation at **7cups.com**.

What's interesting is that a modest hypothesis (that people didn't know what we meant by "Listener") led to a significant improvement, and the subsequent experimentation revealed a further insight (there are people out there specifically looking for opportunities to volunteer).

As you try to answer those questions, the ideas that suggest themselves to you as explanations are your hypotheses, but, of course, not all guesses are created equal, so it behooves you to make your hypotheses crisp and testable, and to have colleagues whom you can discuss or sketch these ideas with and who can be your "thought partners" in refining them, riffing on them, or nailing down the implications.

Because once you have a hypothesis you like, you'll need to come up with one or more experiments you can do to test the hypothesis.

Proposing and Prioritizing Experiments

As you break down the product you work on into components or functional areas, you'll find it's quite possible to generate many hypotheses about each piece of functionality or flow in each area. Ideas are a dime a dozen, and the product manager's job is to provide focus by facilitating prioritization.

For any given hypothesis that you have deemed tackles a serious enough high priority goal, the next job is to come up with experiments to test this hypothesis. Part of this is a matter of logic. If your hypothesis is that there are too many ads on the inbox screen of your mail app, and that this is leading your users to ignore all the ads, an experiment to test this hypothesis might be to reduce the number of ads displayed. If the hypothesis is correct, this should lead to more ad engagement. If not, then there are likely to be other factors at play.

But not all hypotheses are so straightforward as to suggest obvious experiments, and a failed experiment does not necessarily disprove your hypothesis. (It might also be that the experiment failed to test the hypothesis effectively.) So there can also be an element of art or creativity in coming up with experiments that efficiently and elegantly zero in on the "hinge" of the hypothesis to reveal the impact of making the change.

Table 7.1 shows a set of hypotheses paired with experiments that might help prove them one way or another.

TABLE 7.1 A SET OF HYPOTHESES AND SOME EXPERIMENTS TO TEST THEM

Hypothesis	Experiment
People are reluctant to sign up for a service before they know its value.	Provide a way for new users to try the service before signing up.
The "Become a Member" call to action on the primary button sounds like a big commitment.	Change the primary button's call to action to "Get Started."
Data show that 40% of in-app messages go unanswered because logged-out users are unaware of pending messages.	Add a step during sign-up asking the user to turn on push notifications and explaining that this will ensure that they don't miss critical messages.
Without knowing who is behind this service, people are reluctant to trust you with their sensitive data.	Show your team, their academic credentials, and the awards won for building robust privacy-preserving systems on the home page.

Also, hypotheses and experiments are not always one-to-one. You can, and often should, come up with multiple ideas for experiments to test a hypothesis. This may be because you are searching for the angle that most effectively tests and reveals the potential of the idea, and it can also occur when you run a successful experiment and want to go back to the same well to see whether a follow-up experiment will yield further benefits on top of the optimization or success already achieved.

Table 7.2 shows multiple experiments generated as possible ways to test the original hypotheses.

So after you do this for a while, you're going to have a big pile of hypotheses and an even bigger pile of proposed experiments to test these hypotheses, which brings us back to prioritization.

One thing you learn quickly is that you can't test everything. You can't research everything. You can't answer every question or worry you have, and you can't eliminate risk. But reducing risk (or *de-risking* in the jargon) *is* one of the primary goals of experimentation, which means that what ultimately should determine which experiments you run and which ones you put off comes down to identifying the riskiest bets you are considering and doing what you can to mitigate those risk in particular.

TABLE 7.2 TWO OR MORE EXPERIMENTS FOR EACH HYPOTHESIS

Hypothesis	Experiment
People are reluctant to sign up for a service before they know its value.	• Provide a way for new users to try the service before signing up. • Add a video to the home page demonstrating how easy and rewarding the experience is. • Show real customers and real quotations endorsing the service. • Include the logos of all the well-known businesses already using the service, as "social proof" of its value.
The "Become a Member" call to action on the primary button sounds like a big commitment.	• Change the primary button's call to action to "Get Started." • Change the primary button's call to action to "Give It a Try." • Change the primary button's call to action to "Get in There!"
About 40% of in-app messages go unanswered because logged-out users are unaware of pending messages.	• Add a step during sign-up asking the user to turn on push notifications and explaining that this will ensure that they don't miss critical messages. • Send users email reminders when they have unanswered messages.
Without knowing who is behind this service, people are reluctant to trust the company with their sensitive data.	• Show your team, their academic credentials, and the awards won for building robust privacy-preserving systems on the home page. • Publish a white paper about data security to establish bona fides and credibility. • Emphasize the use of data encryption both "in transit" and "at rest" in describing the service.

For example, tweaking the color of a button to try to catch more eyes may be something you can just go ahead and try without testing anything first, because the existing risk of maybe not having the ideal button color is not huge and the downside risk of being wrong is probably also not game-changing.

But now imagine that you have several important goals in tension (which you always do, by the way). Let's say you need to increase growth by juicing sign-ups and improving retention around free services, but you also have a significant revenue stream from impulse buyers that you need to maintain and ideally grow as well. In this scenario, it might be easy to make the option of signing up and engaging in the free services much more attractive and prominent than the impulse-buy call to action, but the risk of doing so is tanking a critical revenue stream. In that case, rushing ahead to make the change feels too risky, and an experiment on a small subset of your traffic can be a good way to study the trade-off before betting next quarter's payroll on a longer-term growth ideal.

One other factor that complicates your prioritizations of experiments is that running more than one experiment at the same time in the same area or flow of your product leads to muddy, hard-to-interpret results. So as long as you are running experiments that don't conflict, you can have several in flight at the same time, up to your ability to keep track and cope.

> **NOTE** LEARNING FROM NETFLIX
>
> To dig deeper in how to conduct A/B testing at scale, check out "It's All A/Bout Testing: The Netflix Experimentation Platform," a post on Netflix's tech blog.

You'll want to both maintain your backlog of hypotheses and proposed experiments and constantly be prioritizing the upcoming tests and tracking the tests you have under way. A completed experiment, whether scored as a win or a loss, should generate some insight into the validity of the hypothesis (or, at least, the efficacy of the experiment). These insights—stacked up over time—belong with the rest of your research findings, likely in a repository or tracking tool shared with UX and data teams.

Whichever tool you use (I like to use an Airtable template, as shown in Figure 7.2), you'll want to develop an agreed-upon rubric for ranking potential experiments and choosing which to prioritize for upcoming sprints. Factors to consider include the following:

- The potential reach of the experiment (how much traffic flows through the area of the test).
- The potential impact of a successful experiment (somewhat subjective, but are you shooting for a 10% improvement in the metric being tracked? 50% 2x? 5x?).
- The engineering and other staff effort required to complete the experiment.
- How confident you feel and what evidence you have to support the hypothesis.

Figure 7.2 shows an Airtable template used to prioritize, track, and score experiments. The template was initially provided to me by product and growth expert Jesse Avshalomov, and it was tweaked over time for various projects and clients. (Airtable is a relational database tool with a fluid user experience, which some product managers find extremely flexible and useful in corralling and tracking complex moving systems.)

Airtable helps you score experiments in terms of potential impact, effort, confidence in the hypothesis and a few other factors. (You can overrule the score when deciding what to do next, but it helps a lot with the broader strokes of prioritization.)

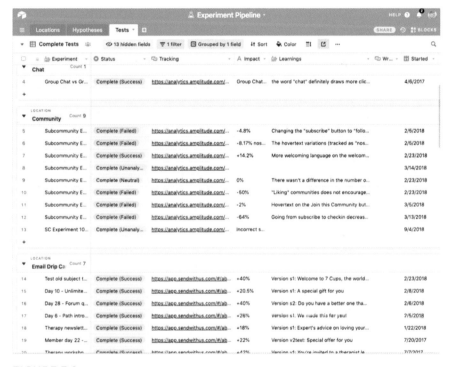

FIGURE 7.2

A glimpse at the experiment pipeline keeping track of hundreds of experiments before, during, and after.

How to Run an A/B Test

You may recall that not all experiments take the form of A/B tests, but it remains a potent tool in your kit, and while the general format of this kind of testing doesn't change much, the specifics of how such tests are managed and implemented varies from shop to shop. Some teams use third-party JavaScript-based tools such as Optimizely, while others use tools built into analytics packages such as Google Analytics, Amplitude, Mixpanel, Applytics, and so on. Still others hand-roll their own tests directly in code (which can lead to problems later if not cleaned up properly).

Factors to consider when running bucket tests (also known as *split test, bucket test, multivariate test, A/B test*) include the following:

- Scheduling
- Statistical Significance
- Impact
- Learning
- Stacking

Scheduling

As with any development work, including building and fixing, running prioritized tests has to be weighed against other items in the backlog and then prioritized into sprints. Tests can in many circumstances run longer than a single sprint, so starting the test, overseeing the test to make sure it is running properly and no bugs have shown themselves, and then ending the test are all distinct tasks that you need to track individually.

The reason that tests take varying lengths of time to resolve themselves is that they don't yield meaningful results until they have included a statistically significant number of subjects. Depending on the traffic flow through the area where you are testing, getting enough people in "each" bucket can take anything from a day to many weeks.

Statistical Significance

So how do you know when you have achieved statistical significance? There are mathematical models to help determine this, and software tools that facilitate A/B testing (such as Amplitude) now include measurements of statistical significance, as well as the likelihood that the result is correct. Note that as a very broad rule of thumb, you tend to need at least 2,000 people in each "bucket" before you can trust a result.

One way to test this result, which can be very interesting, is to run an A/A test. Basically, you set up an A/B test and put new users into one bucket or the other, but you serve up exactly the same experience to people in each bucket. What you'll see early on as the data starts rolling in is that B performs much better than A, or the other way around—no, wait—now it's changed again! Just as you might flip a coin four or five times in a row and get heads every time, if you flip it enough times, the number of heads and tails results will end up nearly equal (unless you are in a Tom Stoppard play).

Keep an eye on your test and note when the results approach parity and stay pretty even from that point on, and don't be surprised if this stabilization takes place when there are about 2,000 people in each group.

It's extremely important to determine when you will end the test before you start it. Otherwise, the temptation is to "cherry pick" by ending the test when the result you are rooting for is ahead. Similarly, you need to end the test when it has reached significance, instead of "just letting it run a little longer" in hopes that your under-dog will still pull it out in overtime.

Impact

After you've ended the test, you have a measurement of its impact. Did more people in the varied bucket do the thing you wanted them to do? Was it a wash? Or did it actually depress the results? Any outcome is fresh information and welcome, but of course winning is better! Either way, you need to track and record these results.

One of the biggest dangers of A/B testing is "polishing a local maximum," which means optimizing something to the utmost degree without realizing that there are much more valuable possibilities out there (Figure 7.3).

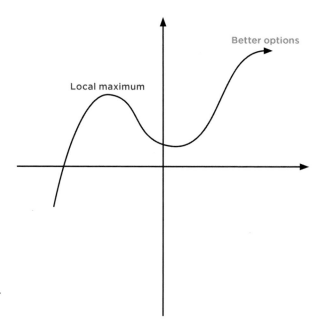

FIGURE 7.3
Polishing a local
maximum can lead to
ignoring much greater
opportunities.

Learning

In addition to tracking the numerical impact on goal metrics achieved by each AB test, you also need to make a qualitative assessment of the meaning of the results. Did they validate the test, partially or in full? Did they reveal a flaw in the hypothesis (or the test itself)? Do they suggest further hypotheses or additional tests to try?

This is part of your product's intelligence arsenal and building that up over time is even more important than "winning" the current tests you're running.

Stacking

It's true that you even learn things from tests that fail to prove the results you were shooting for. Actually, some people will argue that you tend to learn more from failures than you do from successes (although I believe this only holds true if you take success for granted and refuse to examine and reflect on it as thoroughly as you do your failures).

However, winning is better!

And once you have a win, you can end your test and "lock it in." Now instead of just one-half of your users, or one-half of ten percent of your new users, getting the benefit of the improvement found by the test, everybody can get in on it.

Then it's time to see if you can stack some more wins on top of that first one. Was the test as aggressive as possible or did you hedge your bets to avoid disrupting other metrics? Can a further test take things up another notch? If there isn't any easy variation on the successful test to try, what about the other experiments that came afterward in the prioritization stack-rank? Try one of them! In some cases, you can return to the same well multiple times and turn a 20% increase into a 100% increase, or a 5x improvement into a 10x improvement.

The losses teach you something, but those locked-in wins can stay with you forever.

Problems with A/B Tests

A/B tests are the shiny thing that product folks gravitate toward. They seem easy to explain and understand, but they can be misleading and fill you with a false sense of confidence.

Beyond the risk you've already seen of polishing a local maximum, there are several other major pitfalls with relying on this type of testing to make decisions.

Most of them boil down to two major themes:

- There is no way to know for sure if externalities have affected your test and if running the test again at another time under other circumstances would get the same result.
- At best, you know what is happening, but an A/B test cannot by itself tell you why.

The first set of problems relates to overinterpretation. In some ways, a statistically significant test can disguise the guesswork surrounding it. (At least when you have mere "directional" signals, you are forced to be skeptical, to verify patterns, and to investigate potential reasons for the behavior you're seeing.)

The second set of problems involve projecting subjective qualitative interpretations of the data without validating them. As with so many other metrical signals you might have available to you, such as

WHY YOU OFTEN CAN'T RUN A/B TESTS IN ENTERPRISE CONTEXTS

Another issue with A/B tests is that they are not always possible outside of mass-market direct-to-consumer products. As Clement Kao explained when sharing a day in the life of a B2B product manager, not only is the user base of many business products too small to generate statistically significant traffic, but the customers are not anonymous data points but rather specific businesses and people involved in high-touch customer success relationships. "Experimenting" on these customers by showing half of them one interface and half another is a disruptive nonstarter.

Kao said, "In B2B, you can't actually A/B test because someone is trying to use your product to run their business. So if they have to train one cohort of users to use one workflow and another cohort to use a different workflow, you definitely cannot do that. Similarly, it's not helpful to recruit a random 'enterprise user' when you're trying to go after a specific set of customer accounts."

customer satisfaction or net promoter scores, user feedback, ratings and reviews, complaint volume to customer support, etc., the real job is to do your research, interview users, and get deeper into why things are happening the way they are and not just what is going on.

Beyond A/B Tests

Product managers have a bad habit of equating all experimentation with A/B tests (just as some reduce all user experience research to usability testing). Remember that experimentation is woven throughout product work at every level. So, more specifically, what are some other forms of experimentation to consider beyond the ever-popular bucket test?

- Variations on A/B tests
- Concierge
- Wizard of Oz
- Pretotypes
- Smokescreen
- Fake door
- Broken glass (aka Hard test)
- Dogfooding
- Partial rollouts
- Beta programs
- Holdover (aka Holdback)
- Sales experiments
- Process experiments

You can find a nice scheme for organizing these methods in Itamar Gilad's *Testing Product Ideas Handbook* (requires free newsletter sign-up to access) in Figure 7.4. His diagram distinguishes "experiments" from other forms of idea validation, but most of the methods in his Tests stacks are experiments in the sense meant in this chapter.

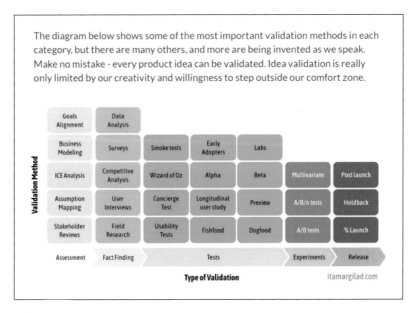

FIGURE 7.4

A good visualization of many forms of experimentation, testing, and validation.

Variations on A/B Tests

Because A/B tests have their limitations, if you're going to use them, you should know the range of related experiments, such as A/B/C tests and multivariate testing. In an A/B test, typically A is the control (the existing experience) and B is the variant tested against it. In an A/B/C test, you split the traffic into three equal-sized buckets and compare the control against two different variations.

A multivariate test is even more complicated. In this scenario, you are trying to test several things at once. To use a trivial example, consider button color, shape, and text. A multivariate test then splits users into sets of buckets. So some users may get the red button with rounded corners that says "Get in there!" and others will get the green button also with rounded corners that says "Start today," and so on. Statistically, this requires even greater traffic to have each of the subtabs (combinations of all possibilities) receive significant numbers, and the interpretation of the results is likely challenging and tricky.

Teams running a lot of A/B tests in flight are often really running disorganized multivariate tests without being aware of it.

Concierge

A concierge experiment is one in which the service provided is not being handled by a software algorithm, but actually by a human being behind the scenes (sometimes an intern).

> **NOTE** TWO SENSES OF THE WORD "CONCIERGE"
>
> *Concierge* is not to be confused with "concierge features," such as a chatbot that helps you find and trigger options in a product.

The role of the person can be explicit or disguised but the point of a concierge test is to learn what customers value and what processes, workflow, language, and other choices work best. Once this is determined, you can get some code written to take the humans out of the service delivery workflow, which will enable the feature to scale up to handle far more people than a manual process could.

If you're up front about it being a human-driven service, as Tom Kerwin puts it, "You get a ludicrous amount of real-world data and experience from having the conversations and solving the problems in real time."

By the way, a related concept that is likely on its way out as terminology is *Mechanical Turk* (not to be confused with Amazon's crowdsourced gig work service), based on an 18th century chess-playing hoax in which an apparent mechanism is disguised as a human operator.

Wizard of Oz

Wizard of Oz testing is just about the same as concierge testing, but it involves providing a convincing user interface and hiding the fact that the back end is just a person typing and performing tasks for the end user.

A start-up called *Aardvark* used this approach to validate its "social search" value proposition, using cheap labor to experiment with robot response strings and to do the manual work of tracking down people in the network who might be able to answer a question. The intern would pose as a bot while texting with both the person doing the search and the person identified who might be able to provide an answer. (They sold the company to Google in under two years.)

Amazon reportedly also used this approach to initially develop their "people also liked" recommendations. They were manual at first, to prove they generated enough income and interest to be worth investing a ton of data and algorithmic development. Zappos launched its entire business this way.

Pretotypes

Coined by Alberto Savoia (as you can see in his talk "Build the Right It"[1]), a *pretotype* is a "fast, low-fidelity version of your concept—be it a product, service, or business—that is just complete enough for you to generate real, data-driven validation. Whereas prototypes answer the question "can we build it," a pretotype addresses "should we build it."

Smokescreen

Not to be confused with "smoke testing" (which means a basic set of functional tests run to make sure that nothing is broken, from the idea of firing up a machine and seeing if it starts giving off smoke), a smokescreen is a promotion for a product that does not yet exist, in order to determine the level of demand.

---

1   www.youtube.com/watch?v=3sUozPcH4fY

You may recall the story of how Jay Zaveri proved there was a pent-up demand for "Word on the iPad" by running ads claiming to have the solution ready. The sign-ups generated by this ad were the result of a successful smokescreen test.

Fake Door

A fake door is analogous to a smokescreen, but rather than being a landing page or sign-up form, it is presented as a real feature in the product's interface. When a customer tries to use the feature, they are instead presented with a promotion for the upcoming feature and sometimes a way to register interest (such as asking to be notified when it's ready). The traffic to this phantom feature is one way to gauge interest.

The risk in this kind of test is that you might frustrate your users.

Broken Glass

Much like an intentional version of the product-market fit assessment, a Broken Glass or Hard test involves offering a feature but deliberately making it difficult to access or use. This is a way of determining if the demand for the feature is strong enough to invest in developing it further.

Dogfooding

Dogfooding, or "eating our own dogfood," means testing a feature in house on your own employees before rolling it out to customers. Google famously did this with a great deal of success for Gmail and with a great deal of failure for Google Plus. Your employees are not always the best proxies for your customers, but one real advantage of *dogfooding* is that it makes it much harder to ignore usability issues and other frustrations when they are hampering your own ability to get work done.

Partial Rollouts

When planning a significant change to an existing product with a substantial user base, a partial rollout allows you to gauge acceptance and adoption and to troubleshoot issues that may not have been presented in research, design, or usability testing.

A common approach is to roll out a new feature first to just 10% of the user base and monitor the response closely. If a problem occurs, roll it back and fix it. If all seems well, then roll the feature out to 20% of your users and repeat. At some point, you may feel comfortable jumping straight to 50% of users and then eventually to all of them.

Beta Programs

A beta program is another way to offer speculative and new features to a core dedicated user group that is willing to test things for you that are not fully baked. Once features are validated, they can be rolled out to non-beta users, and beta users can start playing with even newer feature ideas.

Holdover

A Holdover or Holdback test involves transitioning the product to your new feature or change, but keeping it the old way for a small group of users to keep track of the effects of change over time. As Ryan Rumsey, founder of Second Wave Dive, put it, "The holdover is a nice way to look at performance over time. I think many teams assume an initial test result = same results over time. I've found many features were used initially because they were new, but then dropped back after 90 days."

Sales Experiments

Outside of the product's feature set and user experience, you can apply experiments to other aspects of the value chain, such as sales or marketing. One example of such an experiment is called a *pitch provocation*, which involves trying out one or more provocative pitches to determine which best makes the case for your solution. A pitch provocation takes the form "You've got a big problem, and we can help."

Tom Kerwin said, "It's a way to help tease apart your understanding of possible value propositions and problems. We create several extreme-and-likely-wrong versions of each, and then get prospects/participants to react: to tell us what they think these mean, etc. From that, we can triangulate a better sense of the space."

Process Experiments

Remember that being agile means constantly evaluating how your team is working and looking for ways to improve it. Beyond passively noting process problems and then looking for solutions, you may also consider experimenting with variations in your processes to determine what works best.

As Ryan Rumsey said, you can ask yourself questions such as "What happens with decision-making or velocity when we change our storytelling structure?" and then experiment with those changes to see what impact they have.

If you're ready to embrace experimentation as a way of life, get ready to look at everything through that lens.

A DAY IN THE LIFE OF A START-UP PM

Nicholas Duran, senior product manager at Suvaun, a healthcare benefits upstart

How mature (or how long established) is the organization you work for?

Four years old with start-up mindset

Share anything else that might help describe the environment in which you practice product management.

We are a young company, recently acquired, that is growing a technology platform for a multibillion dollar industry and a captive audience that is largely resistant to change.

How do you spend the early morning?

Typically, I review/update/organize the to-do list for the day and week. I hit urgent items first and then move on to meetings, planning updates, and documentation.

How do you start your workday?

In the a.m., it's the family routine, coffee, more coffee (maybe a quick peek at online news and feeds for noteworthy industry updates), a quick system check for any new tasks, calendar invites, or monitoring alarms. Then a healthy morning stand-up meeting with the team. After that, it is off to the races.

How do you spend most of the morning?

Clearing road blocks and doing correspondence.

How does the morning end?

The ongoing routine and clock blur into a state of hunger. Then a decision is made whether there is time or not to proceed on to lunch.

When do you take a lunch break?

Mid-day is a typical lunch range—anywhere between 11 a.m. and 3:00 p.m. Maybe a 10–15 min step outside for some sun on the face.

What do you do first in the afternoon?

Check email and recover from lunch.

How do you handle "fire drills" or other unplanned work?

Carefully! I check priorities, assess risk, and schedule accordingly. It depends on how severe the issue is.

How do you spend the bulk of the afternoon?

I spend it in meetings, use cases and operational excellence improvements.

What do you do at the end of the workday?

Refill my coffee, update my notes for the next day, check feeds and updates online, check LinkedIn, and thank the team for another great day.

Do you work in the evening?

When necessary. ∎

Key Insights

- Experimentation is a way of life for product managers.
- Building, fixing, and optimizing are all aspects of development you can experiment with.
- Develop testable hypotheses about how to improve results and fix problems.
- For each hypothesis, generate as many ideas for experiments as you can.
- Prioritize both hypotheses and experiments rigorously.
- Use experimentation to "de-risk" your riskiest bets.
- Don't reduce all experimentation to A/B tests.
- Make sure that your test results are statistically significant.
- Be careful not to focus on relatively trivial improvements.
- Stack up your wins!
- Experiment widely, not just with feature variations.

CHAPTER 8

Getting the Money

While it's not true that all designers get uncomfortable when the talk turns to money (budget constraints, the need for revenue, potentially seeing people as paying customers above all else), it's fair to say that many UX designers are happy to have someone else (a "bean counter," a "suit") obsess about grubby stuff like money and find their comfort zone far away from the bazaar and the cash register. Designing shopping carts, check-out flows, and credit card forms is about as close as most people get and that's plenty close enough, as these tasks rarely inspire flights of creativity.

However, my take on this issue is not everyone's. B. Pagels-Minor pushed back on this broad brush, saying, "I generally disagree with this. Many UX designers I work with are just as savvy and thoughtful about how to monetize as many product managers."

It's probably true, and I may be betraying my own narrow experience and some lingering stereotypes that need updating. So, really you can answer for yourself whether you cringe when money is taken into account as a factor in UX design and product development.

Regardless, money is the life blood of our economy, no matter what sector of the economy you work or play in. Of course, there are huge swaths of human endeavor that are not transactional or commercial, but even government, nonprofits, and other types of organizations need resources, spend money, and have to stay afloat somehow financially.

As a product manager or frankly even a product designer, it pays to keep an eye on the money. Design teams are often viewed as cost centers. UX has spent more than a decade arguing that it provides sufficient return on investment (ROI) to justify the research, the modeling, the iteration, the prototyping, and the testing. There's always been an undertow of costs vs. benefits pulling UX along with it. From a product perspective, you're just including this financial dimension in your larger model of what's going on, what you're making, and how you're going to succeed.

Profit and Loss

In a business's C-suite, financial tracking, modeling, and projection are constant. Profit and loss (P&L) responsibilities tend to roll up to division heads and general managers. Heads of product may have P&L responsibilities, but most product managers do not. They don't tend to have decision-making power over hiring budgets or resource allocation, outside of their own product (at best). A PM rarely controls the P&L situation, but it sure can control you, and you need to be aware of it.

Depending on the context and the product's lifecycle, you may be doing business modeling, working out the cost of goods sold, defining revenue targets, and identifying suitable pricing levels. That context might be business, and if so, is it consumer or enterprise? And if not, who is paying for the service, and where do those resources come from and what else might compete for them?

Where the product stands in its lifecycle will drive different financial expectations. Typically, there is a period of R&D and investment launching a product where it generates costs with no revenue or income at all. Later, it will be time to figure out how to get the service paid for without necessarily having to achieve total independence of funding from revenue alone ("break even").

Beyond that a successful product would be expected to more than pay its own way in terms of revenue generated vs. cost to produce and deliver. Some products have long periods of plateauing and maintenance where revenue is steady and optimized but no longer particularly growing or likely to peak again. Finally, at the end of a product's life, when it no longer makes ends meet financially and has no viable future, a PM needs to work out the legal obligations to legacy customers, communicate plans to take it off the market, and ultimately wind things down while minimizing the remaining liabilities on the books.

Revenue Models

Not all products come with price tags directly attached. If you make enterprise software in a B2B context, the customer may have paid for multiple subscriptions to an entire suite of software, and the product you're working on may come as part of that package, whether an individual user ever tries it out or not. This is where SaaS (software as a service) products come into the picture. Now you're offering entire enterprises your software as a hosted turnkey service, at scale, and charging per seat.

SaaS products charge their users much the same as a streaming entertainment service charges you a single monthly subscription fee rather than asking you to pay for each show you watch. It still costs money to make those shows, and you can be sure that Netflix and Amazon Prime pay very close attention to which shows do get watched (and for how long) and how well that correlates with viewers deciding to continue their subscriptions, and so on.

So even if there isn't a point-of-sale transaction, the individual product still bears a measurable relationship to the business model, and its product manager needs to account for that aspect when defining success metrics. (Once these metrics are defined, the growth practices covered in Chapter 6, "Product Analytics : Growth, Engagement, Retention," come into play to try to optimize those metrics.)

For a thorough dive into possible revenue models for products, you may need to go back to business school, but some of the most common ways to bring revenue in for a product include the following:

- Free during a beta period, and then paid for all.
- Free during a trial period, and then paid if not canceled.
- Free during a trial period, and then a paid recurring subscription if not canceled.
- Paid subscription (no trial period).
- Free product with in-app purchases available.
- Free product with offer to upgrade to paid Pro version of product.
- "Freemium" paywall to unlock higher level(s) of service.
- Enterprise licenses paid by seat.
- Enterprise licenses paid by usage.

What works best for your product will depend on the needs, drives, and constraints of your potential customers.

NOTE CUSTOMERS ARE DIFFERENT FROM USERS

> A *customer* is a person who pays for a service. A *user* is a person who uses a service. A user may or may not be a customer, and vice versa.

Your revenue model is another area of potential experimentation, but it can also mean betting your business and your livelihood on your decisions, so this means treading carefully and doing your research up front, as well as studying the data and other signals intently and being prepared to drop a bad model and pivot rather than remaining overly attached to your favorite ideas.

Even when you have found the right model, you'll want to tune it to find the best price points, the right things to put behind the paywall, the optimal subscription rate, and so on.

Breaking Even

Getting a product (or a business) to the break-even point is a tremendous accomplishment. Until you manage that, it's hard to call the effort a success.

Of course, nothing lasts forever. Some tremendously influential and valuable products came and went without ever making a profit, let alone breaking even. Still, if money is the lifeblood of the material world, then getting to the point where you take in more than you lose is, in the long run, just the ante required to play the game at all. What you do next is the real challenge.

For four years, I headed up the product team at 7 Cups, a start-up that had graduated from the YCombinator incubator program, which instills a ruthless honesty about growth metrics and facing up to when they are not growing. At its core, 7 Cups offered a way for anyone on the planet to get emotional support from a stranger anonymously, privately, and securely over the internet, in the form of a text chat. There was more to it than that, but the basic value proposition was peer-based support for free on demand.

FROM THE TRENCHES...

POSTPONING REVENUE IN A LOSS-LEADER STRATEGY TO OWN A MARKET

As a counterpoint to this framing, Netflix product manager B. Pagels-Minor suggested I may be oversimplifying things a bit here, saying "I disagree. Amazon was not profitable for years. Neither was Netflix, and it was well understood that that was the plan. I think saying break even as the success metric is pretty illogical in modern tech companies. It's more likely that the goal would be to get market penetration."

This is a really good point! There are, of course, more examples of companies that won on market capture long before they found a way to capitalize on it. A few dominant products in terms of market share still have not! So, take this as a case study in one particular path and try to see how the same thinking and doing could crack other success goals aside from that of "breaking even."

When I came aboard as VP Product, I could see that 7 Cups already had product-market fit. The user interface was frankly somewhat ho-hum, having already evolved through a series of feature hacks and design tweaks post initial launch. The value proposition wasn't fully clear, and the first-time experience and navigation were something of a maze.

And yet people were "crawling through glass" to seek support (and increasingly to offer it) in growing numbers. Clearly, 7 Cups had tapped into a deep-seated need for authentic caring and connection among people (see Figure 8.1).

FIGURE 8.1

Game of Thrones star Maisie Williams experienced online bullying after achieving stardom as a young actor, and shared in a BBC anti-bullying campaign how she had found anonymous support at 7 Cups.

Making sure that it remained free was also a core part of the mission, and although growth kept increasing, the rate of increase was slowing, which isn't what venture capitalists love to see. (They also really like their pigeonholes, so if they can't decide if you are a behavioral health start-up, a digital therapeutics play, or a social network, they tend to throw up their hands.)

We kept working on growth hacking, of course, but in the meantime finding a VC "sugar daddy" to provide millions of dollars for us to experiment with to find how to keep a business afloat offering free services powered by volunteers was looking increasingly unlikely.

Our early-stage investors were becoming a bit anxious, too, and they suggested strongly that we start looking into ways to generate revenue. So we began a series of experiments, as follows:

Experiment #1: Donations

The first idea my boss, the CEO had, was to ask for donations, or as I called it, "the begging bowl strategy." The reasoning was that we were providing a public good, somewhat like public broadcasting, and that we could ask people to donate to support our mission.

I was of two minds about this.

- We were never going to make enough money to stay afloat just from donations.
- There was nothing wrong with enabling people to give us money.

So we agreed to try it, despite my skepticism about the willingness of ordinary folk to donate to a private business that is not a nonprofit. (This is called "disagree and commit" and is a big part of product leadership.)

We debated whether to enable one-time donations or to require that they be recurring (meaning someone would have to cancel before a month passed if they really wanted to give just once), and we experimented with how to present the option in our user interface, as well as with persuasion or even what you might call *social engineering*.

We created something called the "compassion jar" and asked folks to help "fill it up" every day. It sat there in the menu bar, right next to a user's profile image and user menu (see Figure 8.2).

FIGURE 8.2
Only two donations in the compassion jar so far that day!

Clicking the jar took the user to the donation page. After several people asked for the ability to make a single, sizable donation, we relented and included a one-time donation alternative to the recurring model (see Figure 8.3).

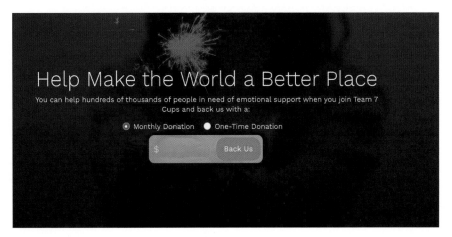

FIGURE 8.3
When a 7 Cups user clicks on the compassion jar, they are encouraged to make a donation (and while it defaults to a monthly option, the donor can now also select a one-time donation).

In the long run, this did generate a small, steady trickle of revenue, what one might call "pin money" or "petty cash," but as I had anticipated in my gut, it was clear after a few months that this donation model alone would never keep the entire business afloat.

By the way, 7 Cups is far from the only business to ask for donations when providing a useful service. Another example I came across recently is Bot Sentinel, which helps you determine whether accounts you interact with on Twitter are bots (see Figure 8.4).

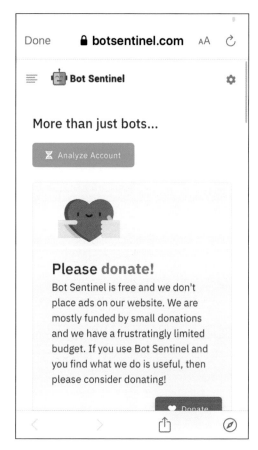

FIGURE 8.4

Bot Sentinel asks for donations, assuming you want to support their mission.

Experiment #2: Upgrades

One of our investors felt very strongly that we could monetize the self-help features of our product, which is called the *Growth Path*. This path comprised a series of steps somewhat like that of another wellness product on the market, Headspace (the mindfulness, meditation app): a series of calming exercises and other bite-sized, self-help experiences.

Headspace used a classic freemium paywall at the time. (The first ten mindfulness recordings were free, and then you paid a subscription to unlock unfettered access to the rest of the library.)

We took a different approach with a basic free path and even a few special paths for people dealing with specific struggles (such as addiction, or anxiety, or bullying, for example), and the rest were "locked" and only accessible to people who paid to upgrade to a premium subscription.

We offered monthly, yearly, and lifetime subscriptions, and we experimented with the pricing and the presentation of these choices over time.

We developed a new onboarding flow that I later called *Yoga onboarding*, which introduced the self-help steps while the new member was waiting for their first connection with a volunteer. This app offered a simple, calming breathing exercise (see Figure 8.5).

FIGURE 8.5
After breathing along with the pulsing sun image for a while, the new member could continue and try another step, if still waiting for a connection.

The new member could continue trying simple steps and gradually come to understand that they were taking a sequence of steps. Eventually, we'd present them with the option of upgrading to get access to a premium path more specifically designed for their needs. Over time, we experimented with when, where, and how to make these offers, as well.

My biggest concern was that we were monetizing a secondary aspect of the product. Our primary value proposition continued to be live, one-on-one chatting with real people. Racking up subscribers to the self-help area wasn't bad per se, but it could lead us to divide our focus and fail to excel in any single area, an omnipresent threat for any product person.

This experiment was somewhat successful. It generated real substantial revenue. By itself, it did not appear even after much optimization to be on track to make us profitable and self-sufficient as a company, but it was definitely extending our runway, and we were learning a lot about what people were willing to pay for, what they valued, and how they felt about recurring subscriptions.

Doubling down on an onboarding strategy geared toward signing up "Growth Path" subscribers for $29/month, we developed our Yoga onboarding design to start with simple steps (breathing, reflection) before feeling committed to a path.

Somewhere along the way, we started our next revenue experiment.

Experiment #3: White Label

Our founder had some experience marketing to universities, and the vast majority of our user base was in the 18–25 demographic, so we developed a white label version of our product to sell initially to schools. This was our first step away from B2C business models. This put us squarely in the world of SaaS.

> **NOTE** DEFINITIONS OF WHITE LABEL AND SAAS
>
> A *white label* product is a generic version of a product designed to be incorporated with an enterprise solution and given the branding of the customer. *SaaS* stands for *software as a service* and refers to enterprise software hosted by the vendor and paid for via subscription.

In some ways, this was a natural fit. Universities and colleges struggle to support their young populations as they experience the incipient mental health challenges of adulthood, pressures from home, coming of age, romantic challenges, and more. Aside from caring for their charges, these schools also have legitimate concerns about attrition and even suicide.

Campus services are both limited in their reach and scope, as well as in some cases all too visible for students or other community members who might feel the need for mental health support as a stigma. An anonymous support service provided through the same sort of mobile chat interface every student has their nose in all day can be a lot less anxiety provoking for anyone concerned about being judged or feeling vulnerable for needing help.

We learned that some schools wanted to use our facilities to enable their own students to provide support for each other, and others welcomed our ability to offer our own volunteers while training their students in our system.

We found we could charge schools' medium-sized annual fees to provide a version of our services to an entire campus or network of schools, but supporting this type of customer also cost us a great deal in terms of resources and focus.

It also raised for the first time the classic product vs. sales confrontation where we had to have "the talk" with our sales reps about not promising product features to close a deal without discussing them with us first! Even with guardrails in place, the reality of larger-ticket customers wanting extra security features, for example, drove our product roadmap in directions different from where it might have otherwise been steered, and worst of all, left us sometimes zigzagging between multiple destinations over short stretches of time.

This white label model looked like it had potential, even with the drag on our consumer roadmap, but it was also not going to grow fast enough alone for us to align our entire business around that model, so we started exploring another avenue for monetization: therapists and professional therapy.

Experiment #4: Directory

While this ultimately came to little as a revenue source, we created a professional directory for therapists, ostensibly competing with the gold standard online directory of therapists, hosted by the magazine *Psychology Today*. We wanted to offer an alternative marketplace for these therapists and saw it as another potential subscription revenue play.

It was a bust financially, primarily because we had insufficient leverage to offer a credible competitive alternative to the established directory. (Famously, if a therapist got one referral a year from their PT listing, it covered their subscription costs. We had no such track record.)

But we did make this directory for an ulterior reason, as a building block toward the next experiment, which was to offer online therapy on our platform. Signing up to offer therapy via 7 Cups would then require that the therapist set up a profile in the directory (see Figure 8.6).

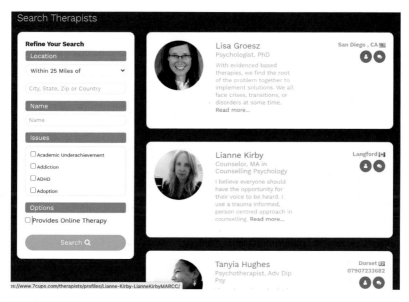

FIGURE 8.6
Therapists in the 7 Cups directory provided another form of support for community members beyond the free service provided by volunteers.

Experiment #5: Paid Therapy

It was time to try another freemium model—professional therapy. This made a lot more sense to me than our attempts to monetize the self-help Growth Path. The classic freemium model offers a core free service and then charges for an enhanced, more fully featured, or higher quality version of that same service.

Here, the idea was that for "free," you could get support from well-meaning volunteers, but also that "you get what you paid for." If you felt you needed or could benefit from a somewhat more highly trained form of support, and that you could afford it, then the availability of a professional tier of service running on the same communications and community platform would enable integrated referrals relatively easily.

The existing community that sustained the free service needed to be included in the discussion about changes and the need for sustenance, and to be reassured that their roles would remain fundamental, and not relegated to a second-class status.

We updated the onboarding again, this time reverting to a chat-first onboarding flow that offered a therapy upsell the first time the new member asked to chat with a person (see Figure 8.7).

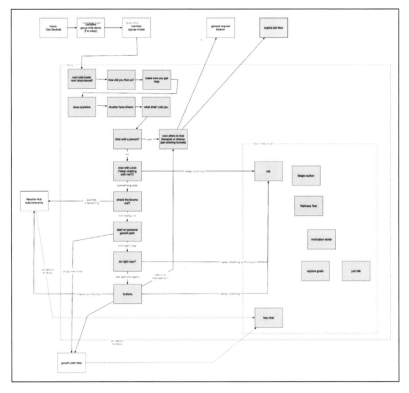

FIGURE 8.7
The 7 Cups onboarding chatbot (Noni) offered an option that would refer a new member to the therapy chatbot (Sophia) to help with sign-up and a subsequent assignment to a therapist.

Therapy Experiments

Therapy showed some promise immediately, but it needed a lot of work. We worked furiously to devise hypotheses and run experiments, holding weekly growth sprints to keep our efforts on a tight cadence.

- We experimented with free trials.
- We optimized the heck out of the sign-up funnels (see Chapter 7, "Testing Hypotheses with Experiments").
- We worked hard on the program design for therapists and the expectations of the therapy service itself.
- We developed dashboards for therapists to show how well they were doing, some of which had counterproductive effects and had to be tweaked or scrapped.
- We experimented with our queueing algorithm that assigned new sign-ups to available therapists.

We stacked up a lot of wins, drove up our funnel conversion rates, and improved our retention of subscribers and support for therapy providers, without unduly hampering growth rates in our free service and community. Eventually, we reached that holy grail of start-ups—the break-even point (see Figure 8.8).

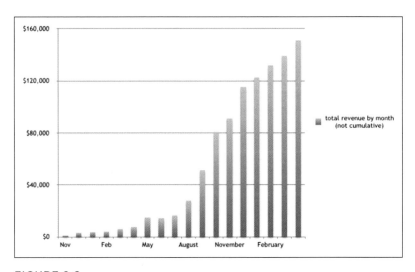

FIGURE 8.8

Fictionalized numbers for illustrative purposes and to protect privacy, but this monthly revenue curve gives an idea of how and when therapy took 7 Cups to the break-even point.

We Were Now "Ramen Profitable"

This break-even point meant that, technically, we were profitable if we brought in one penny more in a month than we spent. If nothing changed, our runway was now theoretically infinite. Well, of course, nothing stays the same forever, and stasis is death in business, but even a temporary reprieve from the wolves at the door is something to celebrate.

Nonetheless, we were profitable in the only way that a lean, volunteer-powered start-up in a mission-driven space could be—by keeping our expenses at a bare minimum, doing everything on the cheap (our motto was "scrappy, not crappy!"), and by paying ourselves well below market rates, which is itself not real sustainability in the long run. In Silicon Valley, this model is sometimes called being *Ramen profitable*.

One way or another, we needed to keep moving forward, but at least now we had some options. Where could we go from here?

There were basically three approaches we could take (see Table 8.1).

TABLE 8.1 THREE DIRECTIONS FOR A BREAK-EVEN PRODUCT

Direction	1	2	3
Name	Where we're going, there are no roads.	The band is just fantastic.	Go for broke.
Description	Grow organically with small bets given theoretically infinite runway.	Optimize LTV/CAG (potential 2–5x improvement possible), raise money, drive lead-gen growth.	Pursue 100x opportunities.

The first direction, "Where we're going, there are no roads," treated the existing break-even business as a platform for experimentation. Within the narrow range of subsistence, it allowed for efforts to find new breakthrough products or even directions to pivot for much greater value.

The second direction, "The band is just fantastic," assumed that the business model that just got the company to breakeven was the best vehicle for making it truly profitable in a healthy sustainable way.

The idea was that doubling down on the value in the core service and paid version of it and using the same fierce honesty toward key metrics that pushed the rock up the hill in the first place would continue to build upon the initial success in a steady, reliable way.

The third direction, "Go for broke," resembled the first one superficially, in that it took the current success as a platform for greater things, but it involved swinging for the fences and looking for breakthrough, game-changing, market-making opportunities, more or less suggesting that if you've managed to figure out a way to get from 0 to 1, there was no reason to assume you couldn't get from 1 to infinity.

Depending on the line of business, the economy, the competition, and a host of other factors, any of these directions might have been the right one for that product, or for yours.

Managing Multiple Lines of Business

It's worth noting that the story of a company with one product getting to breakeven involved experiments with multiple, different business models, and entirely separate lines of business (see Figure 8.9). This is not unusual, and while singular focus has its virtues, multiple lines of business can present packaging opportunities.

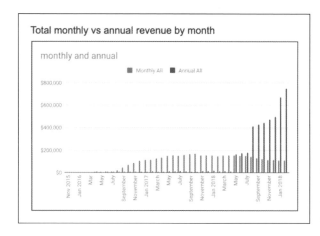

FIGURE 8.9
Fictionalized data (to protect the innocent) illustrates how the layering of multiple lines of business, some with monthly pay cycles and others with annual pay cycles, contributed to the growing revenue for this product.

Revenue Lifecycles

While tales of launching products from scratch, growing a user base, and then finding a way to pay for it all can be inspiring, it's also risky to focus on the initial stages of a product's lifecycle to the exclusion of the ongoing dynamics around revenue, cost, budget, resources, and finance.

A product that has established itself with a set of users and with a relatively secure place in the product roadmap and the company strategy is more likely to focus on sustaining and optimizing existing revenue streams, rather than trying to find something where there is currently nothing. This approach may appeal to product folks with less of a "frontier" mentality. In some ways, these are the banker, supplier, and governance approaches that tend to follow the pioneers.

Eventually, they will reach the end of their run and require "sunsetting" (shutting down). It can be a challenge to recognize and act on this moment, as even dwindling revenue streams are hard to turn off.

Sustaining and Optimizing an Established Product

The underlying mechanisms of sustaining or optimizing an established product are the same. There are fixed costs and costs that scale with use. There are recurring revenue streams and intermittent forms of revenue. The moves are more fine-tuned, though, and more about keeping a well-oiled machine humming, a reliable revenue stream unclogged, and a stable customer base satisfied.

There is a long-term risk of complacency as an incumbent, according to Clay Christensen's famous "innovator's dilemma." It's a dilemma in the sense that incumbents don't fail to innovate just because they are weak or soft or jaded, but because a comfortable, established product *literally* can't afford to innovate. The risk to the existing revenue stream is just too high. This creates the opportunities that upstarts eventually take advantage of, which leads to the third and final stage in the lifecycle of a product.

Sunsetting

All things must come to an end, and digital software products (and the revenue streams and profits they may generate) eventually follow suit. It's probably no product manager's favorite assignment, to preside over the sunsetting and decommissioning of a product that has outlived its usefulness, but this end-stage scenario draws on similar proficiencies sets.

Don't believe me? Here's what you need to decommission a product:

- Identify the decaying profit vs. loss patterns and make the tough decisions about where and when to cut losses.
- Wind down commitments, set expectations, preserve security, privacy, and other legal commitments.
- Ultimately, take a product entirely off the books of a business.

As you can see, this is a mirror image of the skills needed to build up successful products in the first place!

What's Money Without Customers or Transactions?

It's easier to talk about money in terms of transactions, whether paid by a consumer at point of sale or by an enterprise customer via wire transfer, but product management work outside of business still runs on the same lifeblood as for-profit enterprise: money.

Government, nonprofits, other non-sales/business forms of organizations all have bills to pay. Money is the circulatory system of the material world. In a nonprofit, donors and members provide the resources, even if there are no revenues, per se. Software development of new features or fixes to old bugs costs money for governments, just as it does for companies. The money part of the job never goes away, and there is no reason to shy away from it.

As a product manager, once you see the money flowing below the surface of nearly every effort, you'll recognize that in many ways, it is as much a material that you are building with as the lines of code or the pixels on the screens.

A DAY IN THE LIFE OF A FINTECH PM

Michael Curry, head of product at 100x Group, an international crypto (financial tech) start-up

How do you start your workday?

Check Slack and email.

How do you spend the early morning?

Getting coffee and planning out the day on a calendar.

How do you spend most of the morning?

Squeeze as much heads-down individual contributor work in as possible before meetings.

How does the morning end?

Meetings get rolling.

When do you take a lunch break?

12 noon.

What do you do first in the afternoon?

Sometimes coffee again. Take an hour to prepare for late afternoon meetings during Asia morning.

How do you handle "fire drills" or other unplanned work?

Directly and hands on. I help multiple departments plan through incidents and execute.

How do you spend the bulk of the afternoon?

More meetings, followed by documentation and recaps.

What do you do at the end of the workday?

Dinner with family. Help daughter with homework. Put baby to bed.

Do you work in the evening?

Frequently. ■

Key Insights

- Business and revenue are core product responsibilities.
- If you have created a valuable product, you can find a business model to sustain it.
- It's OK to try multiple revenue models.
- Don't be afraid to abandon a revenue model that isn't working.
- It can work to maintain multiple revenue streams at different levels of effort.
- Breakeven is a pivot point for any product where its roadmap is temporarily infinite.
- Financial inputs and outflows drive what's possible for a product at every stage of its lifecycle: establishing, sustaining, and sunsetting.
- Even outside of transactional products, money is one of the materials that a product manager works with.

CHAPTER 9

Healthy Collaborative Tension on the Product UX Spectrum

With it pretty well established that UX practitioners and product managers share many concerns and deploy adjacent proficiencies, this leads to a perennial struggle to define exactly who is responsible for what. There are as many schemes for divvying up the work as there are teams out there, but they are often some variation on this formula:

- The product manager is responsible for "what."
- The UX designer is responsible for "how."

So, problem solved, right? Short chapter, eh?

But, of course, even if we agree on exactly what "what" refers to versus "how," exactly how do you apply a rubric like that in practice? Where do you work separately, on what do you work together directly, how do you coordinate, and who has the final say when you are collaborating?

The Overlap and Its Disconnects

If you remember the product-UX histogram from Chapter 3, "UX Skills That Carry Over," you will recall that there are a number of skills in the middle of the spectrum that could plausibly be handled by a UX expert or a PM, depending on the team and the context (see Figure 9.1).

Branding
UI system creation
Front-end development
Sound and motion
Visual design
Conversational design
Prototyping
Studio critique and iteration
Interaction design
Wireframing
UX writing
Content strategy
Service design
Collaborative design
Sketching
Information architecture
UX strategy
Personas and user journeys
User research
Research synthesis
Stakeholder facilitation
Concept modeling
Usability testing
Customer interaction
Market research
Data analysis
Sprint planning
Backlog maintenance
Bug tracking
North Star metrics
Acceptance criteria
User stories and epics
Roadmapping
MVP definition
Feature prioritization
Revenue modeling
Hypotheses and experimentation
Risk management
Architecture strategy
Product-market fit

FIGURE 9.1

The skills and implied tasks in roughly the middle of the list might fall to a UX person or a product person, depending on the team.

The histogram is a conscious effort to avoid the ever-present Venn diagrams typically used to show overlap and complexity and to help with scoring. However, it can suggest a pronounced linear order or sequence among these skills when their relationships are, in reality, a lot fuzzier. So, when looking at the potential areas of overlap, giving in and plotting some of these skills in a Venn diagram can help illustrate it (see Figure 9.2).

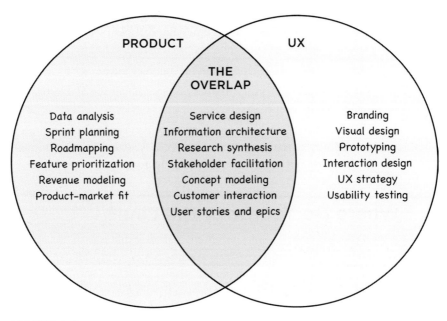

FIGURE 9.2
A sampling of product/UX skills roughly sorted by discipline most likely to do that task.

Abilities and skills shared between colleagues are a good thing, and they cause no problems inherently, but in practice when there is ambiguity about who is responsible for what or who has the final say on what matter, this can lead to conflict, miscommunication, and—most importantly—delivery of poor user experiences.

Conflicts may arise out of a simple lack of alignment or for more sinister reasons. There are definitely people out there who still think in terms of "turf" and try to fend off anyone from any other team or school of thought whom they perceive to be encroaching on their turf. This street-gang mentality isn't great for collaboration, but if it exists, you need to be aware of it if you have any hope of shipping great software with the team you've got.

Aside from outright arguments about who owns a particular project, artifact, or work product, there is also a strong risk of duplication if the product and UX folks pursue their individual agendas in an uncoordinated way.

Each will do research, each will define concepts and models, and each will produce specifications or other design artifacts that attempt to address very similar issues in somewhat different ways, potentially leading to all sorts of problems, including the following:

- Ambiguity at the development and delivery stage.
- Wasted cycles clarifying distinctions that never needed to be created in the first place.
- Endlessly bouncing back and forth between two framings in an infinite loop of a tug-of-war that ends only when someone higher up the chain notices the paralysis on the team.

Where Do You Draw the Line?

A while back, I posted a question to my network that sounds deceptively simple: "Where do you draw the line between product and UX?" Given my contacts in the "it depends" crowd, perhaps I shouldn't have been surprised at how many people tried to reject the premise, questioning whether any such lines exist (or should exist at all).

Most people emphasized the gray area of overlap, which is understandable, given that it is where all the nuance lives, with replies such as:

- "You don't. You enable each other to achieve the best customer outcomes; but to be fair to customers, it doesn't matter if there's a line between product management and design or not." Jeewant Singh Gupta, Product@HSBC
- "The better design leaders think like PMs. Some have crossed over. I know many who aspire to. I'm surprised this isn't talked about more." Dirk Cleveland, Senior Partner at Riviera Partners
- "Are gradients lines? I draw the line at delivery and skillset, but both practices focus on the same thing: delivering results." Eduardo F. Ortiz, CEO Coforma

But lines are not bad things! They can give clarity. It's understandable that people want to avoid sharp boundaries, but this confuses the collaboration layer of work with the decision-making layer.

At the level of working together, yes, of course, let's have no lines. Let's work shoulder to shoulder, looking at the same diagrams and discussing them, handing the marker back and forth to doodle on each other's whiteboard thoughts, writing interview questions and surveys together, but let's also be clear: The product manager has to decide whether the product is ready to ship. The UX strategist has to make the final decision on the navigation taxonomy. And so on. It's not that any of these specific tasks must be owned by one role or the other in the abstract. It always comes down to the specific people involved, not stereotypes, but in each case, these matters of ownership and "final say" need to be clarified, understood, and agreed upon by all involved.

FROM THE TRENCHES...

MATCHING AUDIENCE NEEDS TO BUSINESS PRIORITIES

Adam Connor, VP Design at Rocket Mortgage notes, "Research and design is about needs and possibilities. What are the audience's needs? What opportunities does that create for the organization? What kinds of solutions might meet those needs and opportunities and how would they work?

"Product management is about alignment, prioritization, and progress. What is the org focused on right now? Which opportunities, needs, and solutions does it make sense to focus on right now, given the business's priorities, capacity, and the progress made to date?

"Engineering is about stability, scalability, and enabling. How do you build things so that they're stable and perform well? So that they can be scaled to handle growing audiences and demands? So they are flexible and can be reused as your needs change? And in such a way that doesn't become a roadblock for future technologies and needs?

"The relationships between these things is symbiotic. Each needs the others for both inputs and outputs. It isn't an assembly line of one passing decisions on to the next.

"Each (ideally) is an active participant in the conversations led by the others, not as a limiting factor, but as an enabling one."

As Jeewant Singh Gupta said, "The 'job' for the product manager is driving customer outcomes. As a product manager, anything that improves or impacts customer outcomes matters to me. Whether the design is researched, tested, and developed by someone else or not remains immaterial. As the captain of the ship, I should not just focus on steering the ship, but rather on all the radiators and needles of things that make the ship move in the right direction. If I'm the designer, sure—the line is a beautiful thing—it allows me to focus on things that matter to me from a design outcome and stay true to that."

The Good, the Bad, and the Ugly

Before digging a little deeper into how product vs. UX tends to play out these days, let's take a step back and clarify one point. There is a bit of a gap in the field right now between an idealized concept of fully empowered product management and how the role tends to be practiced in the majority of environments in the breach.

This gap can lead to some confusing discussions when product management is framed in idealized (aspirational) terms. The well-rounded, thoughtful, collaborative, creative, experimental, compassionate PMs described in these books and blog posts don't always seem to match up to the lived experience of UX folks (and others) working with the product people they've got.

There is a risk, too, of falling into the "No True Scotsman" fallacy by excluding anybody practicing product management badly (too rigidly, as an autocrat, without UX savvy, etc.) from being a "real" PM, which is frankly a cop-out.

A better approach is to acknowledge this range of possibilities in practice. There really are honest-to-gosh great PMs out there and well-led highly empowered product organizations fostering many great product teams, but this fully evolved model of product management is still the exception and not the rule in practice across most organizations and industries. (If we're honest, we'll acknowledge that something like this is also true for user experience, and the idealized model of UX research, strategy, and design often falls short in practice when faced with resource, time, and leadership constraints.)

COME TOGETHER ON OUTCOMES

Matt LeMay reframes this in a way that may be more realistic about how role details get nailed down: "I think that on the healthiest teams, the *team's shared outcomes* are clearly defined and well understood. People naturally figure out how to work together toward those outcomes."

You can roughly sort real-world product/UX relationships into three general buckets:

- **The good:** Teams that have healthy thriving collaboration about product discovery and experience.
- **The bad:** Teams where the working relationship between product and UX is faulty and needs work to reach its full potential.
- **The ugly:** Teams that propagate and reinforce toxic relationships among the disciplines.

The Good

The hallmark of a good product-UX relationship is that the roles are clearly defined and well understood by everyone involved. There are many opportunities for collaboration and clearly negotiated "final decision" ownership defined for each shared concern. The biggest challenge here is to preserve this culture as the team succeeds and scales up.

The Bad

The vast majority of product orgs live in this "bad" space where folks mean well, but haven't yet done the work to educate themselves about each other's disciplines, so there is a tendency to miscommunicate or fall afoul of each other's agendas, as well as a tendency to spring "deliverables" on each other.

The opportunity here is to have those difficult conversations. This can start at the individual practitioner level, when a UX designer or product manager or lead from one of those disciplines speaks up and addresses uncomfortable or awkward truths. When everyone can share how they wish things worked and what they are afraid of, it's usually not too hard to find alignment around shared goals and interests and to surface, discuss, and come to "working agreements" around the thus-far mismatched priorities.

Working agreements can be thought of as the social equivalent to Agile's "rough consensus and running code." You don't have to get it all right in one go. That's highly unlikely. But you can work out—for now—some ground rules that are acceptable to all involved. These don't have to be ironclad unchangeable rules. You can work out a rough consensus and give it try. Then you can use your product mindset to retrospectively review and iterate on these working understandings. Together with your counterparts, you can improve these initial agreements through honest airing of what is working well for whom and what is not, which practices are enabling people to show up at their best, and how well the working agreements handle those inevitable days when any of you are not able to be your best.

Individuals can only do so much. One thriving squad can function as a "bright spot" and an example to others, but to really evolve an entire product organization (no matter the size), at some point you need leadership that is committed to working through these difficult conversations at every level. In a mature org that is finally ready to face these challenges, this may require something like time set aside at a company offsite or a special "Product/UX Summit" occasion with all the personnel involved together, or in the cases of very large entities, a representative sample.

The Ugly

There are, of course, many "feature factories" out there, too, where people with product titles function more as project managers (at best) or overseers at worst, driving technical and design teams in a command-and-control environment with little agency, let alone opportunities to reframe questions, align projects with overarching goals, or appeal to product vision or organizational values.

One solution for a UXer or budding product manager in such a toxic environment is to run away. Get out of Dodge. Get a job that nurtures you. But that is easier said than done as often as not, and even if you are actively seeking a better opportunity, you may still need to survive and operate in an ugly product environment for weeks and months before escaping to the promised land.

So what do you do?

First of all, you pick your battles. If you go to total war over every offense large and small against user-centered design or product sense, then you will make enemies and end up either frozen out and told to mind your business or shown the door.

Generally, your best bet is to choose when and where to hold your ground and in those scenarios, use all of your craft skills to communicate why the approach being foisted on you will not work.

Do some research, even when you are told to skip that phase. Get some data that hasn't been cherry-picked to advance one PM's roadmap item over another and make a case for an alternate approach. Just as the devil can quote scripture with the best of them, data selected to shape a narrative or win an argument will lead you down the path to ruin, no longer helping you see what is really going on and instead reflecting back to you a fun-house mirror that you hope you can persuade other people to take for reality.

When overruled, make sure that goals are defined and metrics tracked and ask for accountability when decisions are proven wrong by the outcomes. None of this will be fun, but it can give you some room to further your own practice with integrity until you can find a more supportive environment.

Where in the Org Chart?

One matter that can complicate the product/UX relationship is an org chart. Does UX report to product, or are they peer disciplines? Or a little bit of both? That is, are there UX people and product managers reporting to a head of product (or VP product, CPO, director of product, etc.), but functioning as peers at the individual contributor level? In this latter scenario, does that head of product have experience outside of product management?

As noted previously, engineers rarely report to product managers, although it's not impossible. Engineers also tend not to report up into product org hierarchies run by a product head, but again this is not unheard of. Still, there does seem to be a much greater willingness to subordinate UX and design "under" product than there does for engineering.

Caio B. Nishihara, who is a design lead at Ambev Tech said: "It's common to see UX reporting to product (as well as many other variations of reporting or independent areas) but surely if the company sees design as a strategic driver, then it should keep it out of the product report line to simply avoid 'top-down effects.'"

If you go down the road of becoming a product manager and become a lead, you will eventually find yourself revisiting these questions: Is this your chance to finally make UX a full peer discipline? Can you recruit a counterpart and devolve the team to them? Or by this time, as a product leader who "knows your UX," will you start to think maybe there's nothing wrong with you keeping both of them in your portfolio?

In the end, it behooves you to focus less on how the lines of reporting are officially structured and to focus more on the relationships with your adjacent colleagues. Does it really matter if you both report up to a product director or if one of you reports to a UX director and the other to a product director?

When You're Not a Designer Anymore

One caveat about shifting from a UX career to a product career is adjusting your self image and accepting not so much that you are not a designer any more (feel free to design things in your spare time!), but that you are not the designer on the team anymore. Many a UX-rooted PM has fooled themselves into thinking that the UX people they work with should welcome their design suggestions because, you know, "they're also a UX designer."

Except you're not. You took a different job.

You're entitled to opinions. You can even share suggestions and design ideas. But tread carefully! Just as a client may interpret a wireframe literally despite all your pains to make it clear that it's not "the final design," so, too, does a design "suggestion" from a product manager who fancies themselves to still be a designer come across as a little too fully baked or, worse yet, as a command.

THE AUTHOR'S TAKE

When I have had to function as an art director in partnership with
a UX designer or manager, I have tended to bend over backward
to speak in terms of the problem space and possible approaches.
If I feel the need to sketch an example to communicate an idea,
I "hang a lampshade" on what I'm doing to make it clear I am
illustrating a concept alone, and not offering a tactical solution
or user-interface suggestions.

Being a Hybrid

If you consider transitioning over time from a UX practitioner to a
product manager, or even if you just continue to work in a digital
product context, you may find an opportunity at some point to take on
a dual role. This tends to happen at start-ups or on small new teams
being incubated inside larger organizations. Both of those scenarios
favor people with a wide range of skills and the flexibility to apply the
right tool to the right problem for the right amount of time.

In scenarios like this, you are still the designer, and it might sound
ideal, but in reality, it's incredibly difficult because these really are
two separate jobs. Doing any two jobs at once is a lot of work, not
to mention the overhead of constant context shifting and having to
back up and refresh your working memory. Worse yet, you can't have
honest disagreements with a peer because you are both people. How
do you sort out a really tricky question where one solution provides
a better user experience at the cost of sacrificing a different product
priority? You already know what you think. Challenging yourself is
harder than it sounds.

Still, such roles are a golden opportunity to start establishing both
disciplines in ways that are aligned and compatible with each other.
If you succeed and your team scales up, you can prioritize bringing
in a peer as soon as possible so that you can focus on the role that
suits you best.

SYSTEMS THINKING FOR CONTEXTUAL AWARENESS

Another perspective that crosses this same spectrum is service design. Kristen Ramirez, senior user experience designer at Procore Technologies, puts it this way:

"We don't necessarily have all the tools. At the same time I'm coming from UX, I'm doing UX really well. I'm doing more research, I'm doing more service design. And I think there's a crossover there, too.

"I need to understand a business process because I need to develop the application to support it. If I don't understand what people are trying to do, then I'm not going to make a very good application.

"One of the sites that I worked on was the Uber developer site. All of their enterprise data needs to be accessible and people need to know how to get to it. There were a lot of moving parts with that! It wasn't just 'how does someone do this,' which is one of the things, but really 'how do all these objects relate to each other?'

"Coming from a design background, trying to speak technology to a developer, there's a lot you have to learn that you're not going to be able to learn just by talking to someone.

"You need to kind of be able to model it, to really say, 'I don't think I totally understand these bits. Let me try to draw something for you to show these relationships.' That's what I'm always about: trying to pick up the languages of other people that I work with.

"I've done a little bit of development in my past, front end. Not anything compared to the front end these days, but that still does wonders for working with the development team. I know that this is going to be weird or this is gonna be hard, or I'm going to have to ask questions about this thing. I think it's the same for business. That was where service design was able to give me that bridge.

"It's really an operations problem, although the design is hopefully part of the solution. If you don't understand the whole ecosystem, you're going to pigeonhole your design."

Superfriends

I hope it doesn't sound naïve to suggest that we are on the verge of an incredible blossoming of product experience collaboration. The two concerns are so closely joined together and with a modicum of coordination and communication—two things that both product managers and UX people always claim to be good at—there's no reason why they can't be flowing together in a high-performance dance that multiplies one another's impact in an ever compounding cycle of user-obsessed awesomeness.

Key Insights

- There's no one answer to where you draw the line between product and UX.
- Nonetheless, each team does need to do the work required to draw these lines.
- Lines don't prevent collaboration, but they clarify who decides what.
- Well-run product teams work through potential conflicts and establish well-understood agreements about who is responsible for what.
- In a toxic product environment you need to pick your battles, document goals and metrics, and look for points of leverage (while planning your exit strategy).
- UX may report to product, but this doesn't really change the communication and collaborative effort required to achieve alignment.
- A product manager with a UX background is not a UX designer and shouldn't pretend to still be one.
- Hybrids are both product managers and UX practitioners. This sounds like a dream gig, but it's more of a *frankenjob*.
- There's really no reason why product and UX folks can't soar together.

Roadmaps and How to Say "No"

"That's a great idea," I remember telling a Ph.D. with deep expertise into human interaction who was working at the time in the innovation lab of a huge tech company. "I love it, but how are you going to get it onto the roadmap?"

If you ask enough UX people what it is the product manager has control over that they wish they had more say in, one thing you'll hear about a lot is the *roadmap*. For the product manager's peers and ordinary stakeholders, the roadmap can represent an opaque and even arbitrary lockbox that prevents them from getting the feature or design they want into the product.

For the product manager's upper management, the roadmap often represents a commitment to deliver specific features on specific dates and a source of angst, disappointment, and constantly reset expectation.

Some of the more common things you'll hear about a product roadmap from people in a tech company (including the product managers) are variations of these questions:

- "Where is the roadmap?"
- "Is the roadmap up-to-date?"
- "Where are we on the roadmap?"

So, a roadmap is obviously a metaphor, but for what? What does it actually mean? What's the car, what's the road, what's the destination, and what are the rest stops? Maybe let's park the car on the shoulder and look this thing over calmly to figure out what exactly a roadmap is trying to tell you.

Defining the Roadmap

The songwriter Mose Allison once wrote "Everybody's crying mercy, but they don't know the meaning of the word." So, too, will you hear everyone talking about roadmaps but very few people agreeing on exactly what a roadmap is and what it's supposed to do.

What Is a Roadmap?

As the metaphor implies, a roadmap is a plan for the "road" ahead, a map of where you hope to take your product, feature, or line of products. In some ways, it's more like the old "TripTik" that AAA still puts together for you to customize your road trip with just the stretches of highway and surface roads you'll need to cover to get to your destination.

So what is the destination, in this metaphor? It turns out that is often the source of confusion. Inside a product team, a roadmap helps identify (and build consensus around) what to build now, what to plan for now to build next, and what to plan for next. It provides a way of tracking whether efforts are focused on the most important goals and if adequate progress is being made along the way.

Outside of product teams, most people view a roadmap as a commitment to ship specific features on certain dates in the months and years ahead, but this is a dangerous misconception that causes endless grief for product teams and equally frustrating disappointment for outside stakeholders.

A Roadmap Is Not a Launch Plan

The biggest problem communicating about roadmaps is inevitably stakeholders interpreting it as a launch plan. If the roadmap suggests that you'll be adding the new "Post to TikTok" feature to your cooking app in Q2 and July rolls around without the feature shipping, it's understandable that people are going to interpret that as a failure and a broken promise.

They may have built launch plans and a marketing campaign around this feature. They will be less likely to trust your predictions and commitments in the future, and they may invest less in supporting your feature launches in the future to minimize risk from a "once burned, twice shy" perspective.

By the way, the solution to this problem is to make actual release and launch plans in collaboration with your sales and marketing teams, and include in it only things you actually can commit to shipping and only when you can commit to real dates. When people treat the product roadmap like a launch plan or complain that it doesn't look like a Gantt chart (see Figure 10.1), give them what they want but just keep clarifying that the project plan to ship a specific feature or set of releases on a schedule is a different artifact from the roadmap.

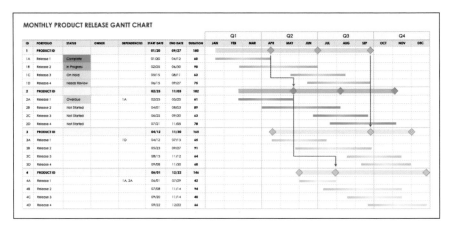

FIGURE 10.1

If your stakeholders need a release plan, give them one, as shown in this Smartsheet template, but at the same time clarify that this is *not* a product roadmap.

Feasible Horizons: Now, Next, Later

A launch plan is anchored to fixed dates with dependencies running backward along a critical path. Wearing a project management hat, you can drive a team toward a launch, trim where needed to keep on track, detect and resolve problems in time, or negotiate new dates with sufficient advance warning when reality intervenes versus your best-laid plans.

A roadmap, by contrast, is a forward-looking document used to prioritize (primarily) near- and medium-term efforts. It is best structured into three rough time frames that can be viewed as a receding horizon getting less sharp as it gets further away: Now, Next, and Later (see Figure 10.2).

Now

Ideas in the Now bucket are things that your team is actively working on currently. This tends to mean things your developers are working on, code you are writing, things you are trying to ship (as opposed to ideas you are still just "noodling" with), etc.

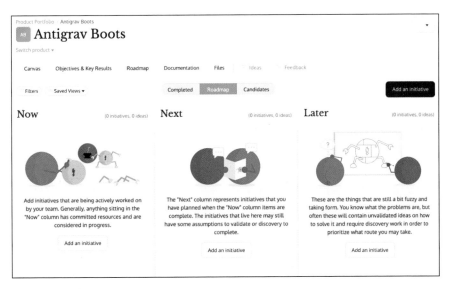

FIGURE 10.2
This empty product roadmap template (using ProdPad) has three main columns, one for each time frame.

Next

Items in the Next bucket are "on deck," as they say in baseball. They are the things you hope to work on next, once the things you are working on now are done. Ah ha, you say! No idea is ever done! True, but the ideas in these buckets are expressed in achievable chunks, and a specific product or feature may be the subject of an ongoing series of ideas.

Developers are usually not actively working on (or preparing to work on) the items in the Next bucket except occasionally to provide some technical ballast for planning and ideation sessions. On the other hand, product managers and UX designers generally are working on these ideas (or their precursors) with stakeholders, so that by the time there is room in the Now bucket, the ideas are ready for developers to work on them directly.

Later

Things in the Later bucket are important ideas that the team is building toward but not ready to work on actively. They may be too speculative at this time, or too dependent on executing Now items or even some of the Next items as well. It's not really worth anyone's time to research, design, or architect these items, beyond capturing the idea as accurately as you can at this time. Then, when there is room in the Next bucket, the team can really start digging in to explore these ideas.

Product Strategy

OK, none of this sounds like rocket science so far, you may be thinking, *but what goes into each column?* Or maybe you're not asking yourself because you think you already know and the answer is *features,* but that's not it.

A product roadmap is *not* a list of features.

Features (or bug fixes, or experiments, or any other changes you ship to your codebase) are (tentative) solutions. They are the results of your research, design, and development work. What you learn after releasing a feature feeds back into your research in the endless build, measure, learn cycle.

So it's a mistake to jump right to features and start dropping them onto a plan. Not only does it lock you into specific solutions before you've done the work, but it also sets concrete expectations with stakeholders leading them back down the path of seeing your roadmap as a release plan.

So what do you put in the roadmap? Outcomes, organized into themes, that are laddering up to company objectives.

Outcomes

You don't put features in your roadmap, you put outcomes. Results. Things you want to happen, such as:

- Double retention
- Increase customer satisfaction by 50%
- Support user requests for more ways to collaborate with each other
- Improve performance
- Reengage with formerly active users

There might be any number of strategies for achieving the outcomes listed (made up) above, and any strategy might suggest a number of tactics worth trying. One of these tactics might be a feature that you might design, build, and ship, but there's no need to lock yourself into a specific narrow, *potential* solution now. It's better to describe what the successful outcome you want looks like and then let the team figure out how to get there.

Organized into Themes

Defining a set of themes to organize and associate outcomes helps keep things aligned, balanced, and legible. It helps you avoid having to sift through a completely random bucket of outcomes, and it provides a framework for recognizing that thematically related goals and initiatives often require an ongoing series of efforts that will span multiple quarters.

It may be tempting to structure roadmap items in terms of the specific product area or functionality they relate to, but "sign-up," "sharing," and "profile management" aren't themes. They are segments of your product. There's nothing wrong with tracking this metadata and even indexing or sorting it, but it's not the right way to organize your roadmap by default.

Themes tend to cluster around related *goals*—such as user growth, retention, revenue targets, network effects, behavioral patterns, and others—defined in your product strategy with the aim of fulfilling your business strategy (or, if you are in a non-business sector, your organization's overarching strategy).

Laddering Up to Company Objectives

This nesting of strategy is key to product alignment. The organization has goals: long-term goals, goals for this year, goals for this quarter or half. The product team within the organization therefore owns some of the responsibility for helping the org achieve those goals.

If you're in a product-centered org, then the product team may be driving most of the overall strategy.

At the leadership level, the head of product coordinates with the rest of the executive team to negotiate commitments the product team can make to the org as a whole in order to fulfill larger objectives. Many tech companies use OKRs (Objectives and Key Results) as a framing device for:

- Articulating clear objectives (basically the same as goals or outcomes)
- Identifying key results that are measurable and can either confirm or falsify whether the goal was achieved, or in the case of goals that can be achieved in whole or in part, measure to what extent the goal was achieved
- Aligning OKRs up and down an organization so that the objectives of any given team fulfill the key results of the team or leader they report to, all the way up (and down) the chain

Owning the Roadmap, or Part of It

If you are the head of product (congratulations!), then you probably own the whole roadmap. If you're anyone else in the product org, then you probably own just a piece of it. (If you're junior enough, you may not actually own any of it, but you will at least be included in discussions about plans for the part of the product you are currently working on.)

For example, a large product organization might have the following levels of ownership laddering up to the roadmap:

- A product portfolio consisting of several lines of products owned by a Chief Product Officer
- A line of products owned by a VP of Product
- A specific product in a line of products owned by a Product Director
- A major piece of functionality (onboarding, administration, core experience, etc.) owned by a Group Product Manager
- A feature owned by a Product Manager
- A backlog owned by a Product Owner

More often than not, outside of enterprise tech companies, you will not have that many levels of articulation and ownership, but the conceptual gradations exist at any scale.

In such larger organizations, the demand for product operations (or "product ops") starts to grow to manage the orchestration of multiple lines of business all trying to make use of the same product and development resources, and this alone can become a complex part of the roadmap planning process.

So let's say that you do own at least some piece of the roadmap; that you are thinking in time horizons of Now, Next, and Later; you're aligned with your team on the major themes in your product strategy, and you've got a nice big backlog of great ideas for how to achieve important outcomes across all those themes.

How do you determine which idea goes in which bucket? This is a matter of prioritization, something that you are responsible for driving and achieving alignment on across all stakeholders, even if you are not empowered to simply make all the tough calls yourself directly.

Converting the wishes and ideas of an org into a clear, usable roadmap is a fundamental responsibility of the product team, and it doesn't ever come easy.

Prioritization

Products are more than just a bundle of features and bug fixes, and roadmaps are more than just a giant wish list.

The product practice sits at the nexus of every input into, and every stakeholder of, the customer experience that represents your company's brand. Product people shoulder the difficult but critical responsibility of weighing the opportunities (and risks) and forging a consensus that moves the team forward and helps deliver valuable outcomes.

There will always be a surplus of great ideas, new problems, ongoing unaddressed issues, deep-pocketed partners, eager sales efforts, business fads, and competitive setbacks. There will always be too many good ideas to do them all at once, without even getting into the opportunity costs involved in each or the fact that many good ideas are mutually incompatible. For example, you can't have two top priorities. You can have any number of important things that you think matter, but only one of them can be the top priority (and if not, then you have zero top priorities, not two).

Weighing these priorities, wishes, good ideas, problems, etc. against each other is a fundamental product practice that takes place at every level of the business. Whoever speaks for product in the C-suite will ultimately decide what the entire product org or effort focuses on, what gets funded, who gets hired, headcount, and so on.

Product leadership needs to address and respond to the business strategy through a product roadmap and operational plan. Product practitioners need to make hard choices about what to ship, what to work on next, the order of the backlog, the priority of bugs, and so on.

Prioritization Methods

It's important to tackle prioritization in a systematic way. There is no one single ideal prioritization method or process or exercise that will suit every occasion and context, but there are always too many good ideas to go around. Stakeholders with varying degree of insight and claim over outcomes all need to be understood, respected, and addressed, and a transparent open process for weighing and evaluating priorities works best.

The most common prioritization methods involve weighing the effort to execute an idea against the potential impact of doing so. In its simplest form, all ideas can be rated as high or low effort and then high or low impact. This approach enables a first-order rough sort. High impact, low effort things go first! Low impact, high effort things never happen. The other two categories then require more careful orchestration to balance the longer term and larger efforts that may yield profoundly good results against the drumbeat of relatively trivial or tactical tasks that are easy to do but won't "move the needle."

Impact vs. Effort

The next level of sophistication for that process is to use T-shirt sizes for estimates (small, medium, and large or S, M, L), which gives you another point on each scale. Most commonly, a large surface such as a wall is cleared to enable an X- and Y-axis with Y (vertical) for impact and X (horizontal) for effort. The same logic applies at all of these scales: the stuff farthest in the high impact/low effort corner comes first, and it's the diagonal in the middle that requires the most scrutiny.

For more complex decisions, use frameworks such as RICE (reach, impact, confidence, and effort). This model keeps the concept of effort and impact from the simple one above, but also gives you a variable to scope the reach of the idea (is it going to impact all of your customers all the time? new users? a subset of existing users? etc.), as well a variable to capture how confident the estimate (or the consensus of the group) is, relative to other ideas.

This latter factor helps address the subjectivity of a quasi-algebraic scoring model such as RICE, but ironically does so by introducing an additional subjective variable.

Important vs. Urgent

Impact vs. effort builds on the concept of the Eisenhower matrix. The Eisenhower matrix is a two-by-two grid that divides tasks, projects, or goals first by whether they are urgent or not, and then by whether they are important or not. The great advantage of this analysis is that it prevents you from confusing urgency for importance (and vice versa).

It is far too easy for anyone at any level of an organization to become reactive to urgent interruptions, emergencies, crises, deadlines, launch dates, publicity schedules, quarterly reports, and so on. It is not possible to avoid urgent priorities, and, of course, most urgent things need to be addressed. But keep in mind that not everything that's urgent is important, and not every urgent thing needs to be handled at the highest level.

More critically, there are many important things that are not urgent in the sense that they are not due immediately and they are not blocking anything right now but are being postponed. The great risk then becomes that these things never get addressed (or, more likely, only ever get addressed when they become urgent, generally by way of catching on fire).

This analysis reminds you to plan and schedule longer term and slower-burning matters so that they come to fruition when they are needed, and you escape the "take-a-crisis-number" method of planning that is more akin to a panic attack than a sustainable execution process.

The Eisenhower matrix (Figure 10.3) reminds you to do those things that are urgent and important immediately, and decide when important things that are not urgent need to happen (schedule them). It tells you to delegate the things that are urgent but not important to you directly, and to delete (forget about) the things that are neither urgent nor important enough to ever be worthy of your attention.

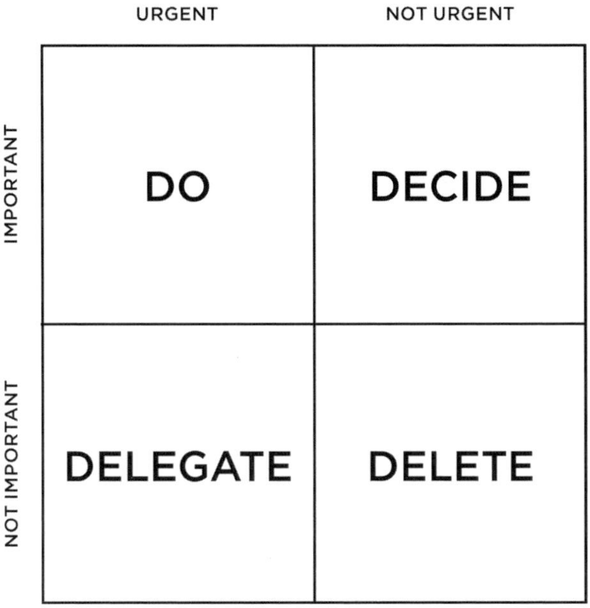

URGENT   NOT URGENT

IMPORTANT

DO   **DECIDE**

NOT IMPORTANT

DELEGATE   **DELETE**

FIGURE 10.3
The famous Eisenhower Matrix helps you plan ahead for important things that are not literally on fire at right this exact moment.

This sort of analysis helps with the broad sorting of goals and ideas into priorities and helps minimize wasted effort and falling into reactivity, but it's not really granular enough for most roadmap prioritization needs.

OK, So Back to Impact vs. Effort

Another two-by-two grid (or *magic square* as some business consultants seem to want to call them) compares impact vs. effort. This is the bedrock trade-off that lies at the core of most product decisions and requires you to think things through along these lines:

- How much value are you likely to derive from doing this thing?
- How much work will it take for the team to pull it off?
- What are the opportunity costs of doing *this* thing and therefore not having time to do *that* thing?

Plotting impact vs. effort helps clarify these points. Sometimes, particularly when facilitating workshop-type sessions with a large group of stakeholders, it makes sense to use a Cartesian plot (X- and Y-axes) and actually rank each item against both scales (see Figure 10.4).

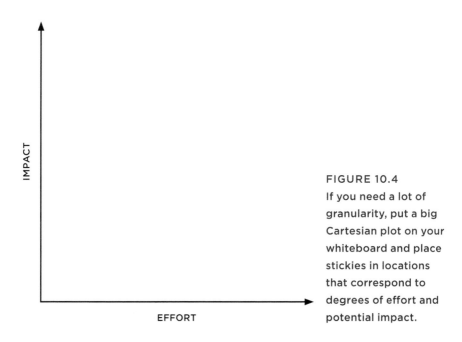

IMPACT

EFFORT

FIGURE 10.4
If you need a lot of
granularity, put a big
Cartesian plot on your
whiteboard and place
stickies in locations
that correspond to
degrees of effort and
potential impact.

Generally, though, you don't need to focus on assessing precise
relative effort or impact estimates between pairs of ideas, so much as
roughly sorting them into four buckets by defining the impact and
effort of each item as either "high" or "low" and then placing them in
the quadrant that corresponds to that intersection (see Figure 10.5).

HIGH IMPACT LOW EFFORT	HIGH IMPACT HIGH EFFORT
LOW IMPACT LOW EFFORT	LOW IMPACT HIGH EFFORT

FIGURE 10.5
Sorting ideas into these
four buckets helps prioritize them at a high level.

Once you sort your ideas into these buckets, then—as with the Eisenhower matrix—you can take a different tack with each of the four categories (see Figure 10.6).

FIGURE 10.6

Drop everything and do those high-impact, low-effort ideas!

1. Definitely do high-impact, low-effort things. They should be the "no brainers" at the top of your list.

2. Meanwhile, review the ideas that would be high impact but would require much effort. You can't do all of these things, but you should invest effort in some of them (as with the non-urgent but still important items in the Eisenhower matrix).

3. Just maintain basic quality control through housekeeping, fixing, and tackling low-effort, low-impact items when convenient.

4. Immediately *delete* and spend no more brainpower or cycles on things that would require high effort without promising anything more than low impact.

Figure 10.7 shows some ideas sorted into an impact vs. effort matrix for an imaginary product.

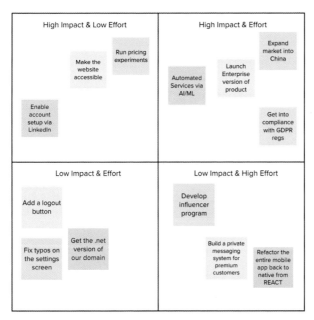

FIGURE 10.7 Without being too obsessed with positioning, the stickies are placed in the squares roughly relative to each other (with higher impact going higher up vertically and higher effort items going further to the right) in each square.

As noted earlier, when estimating effort, another useful rough sort is called T-shirt sizes (typically meaning small, medium, and large, usually abbreviated to S, M, and L, but sometimes extended with things like XS, XL, XXL, and so on). This method is great when planning a sprint, but in a two-by-two matrix, medium impact or medium effort items still have to be forced into a small or large bucket, even if you want to show them hugging the edge.

So...Many...Frameworks

If you start digging into prioritization frameworks, you are going to discover quickly that there are an infinitude of them. Many of them are good! It helps to be conversant with multiple approaches partly so that you have a toolkit that you can adapt to different types of prioritization scenarios (What should the squad work on next sprint? What should the team build next quarter? What are the product goals for the second half of the year?), and partly so that you can adapt to the prevailing methods when joining an existing team.

FRAMEWORKS HELP YOU COMMUNICATE

Matt LeMay said, "I like to think of all of these as communication frameworks. The framework won't help you make a perfect decision, but it will help you communicate how you made a necessarily imperfect decision."

Andrea Saez of ProdPad's "What is the best framework to prioritize what to work on next?" published at Product Manager HQ offers a great overview of prioritization methods and how to know which approach to use when. She boiled her advice down thusly:

> Prioritization is not a linear process, and happens at different stages of development. Start with your objectives, find problems to solve, and run discovery to better understand how different items may give you the desired outcome. Frameworks help you understand and visualize information, foster conversations, and discussions. They are not there to make decisions for you.

A great next step beyond simple impact vs. effort, for example, is the RICE framework, which also brings into account two further dimensions, "reach" (R) and "confidence." (C).

- **Reach** means the potential audience impact of the idea (similar to the traffic dimension of the experimental pipeline prioritization engine discussed in Chapter 6, "Product Analytics: Growth, Engagement, Retention"). When you consider this, it can help you calibrate ideas against each other (since a big impact with a smaller audience may not actually be bigger than a smaller impact with a bigger audience).

- **Confidence** is a percentage used to challenge how sure you are about your assessments of the potential reach, impact, and effort. It gives more credit to ideas supported by evidence.

Populating and Maintaining the Roadmap

OK, but what happened to the roadmap? Well, the end result of all that prioritization, remember, is to place ideas within time horizons to figure out what to work on now, what to prepare to work on next, and what to keep an eye on for later (see Figure 10.8).

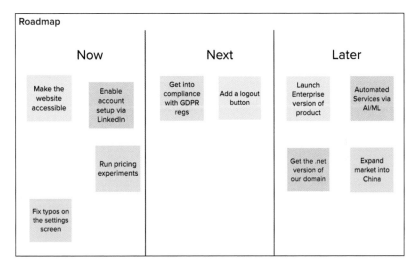

FIGURE 10.8
The ideas sorted by our imaginary product team placed on a thematic roadmap with relative time horizons.

As a product manager, you're really recommending what should go on the product roadmap and where. When you (or your team) presents the roadmap to leadership, it needs to obtain their buy-in, or you'll be sent "back to the drawing board" to try again. So the roadmap is also a proposal or a position in an argument.

When There Is No Roadmap

If you are making the first roadmap, congratulations! You have a blank slate. You'll need to gather input from all your sources and signals, assess them, prioritize them, obtain buy-in, and then communicate the plan to all stakeholders. So, mission accomplished?

Not quite. That's just the beginning. Maintaining a roadmap is an ongoing responsibility.

Keep a Roadmap Fresh

There is a tendency to make a roadmap and then set it on a shelf and only refer to it when the quarter ends or when the board is demanding an update, but this defeats the purpose of planning anything. Instead, you need to revisit the roadmap (or your bit of it) on a regular schedule:

- On a monthly basis (if not each sprint), review the current workload of your team against the roadmap and make sure that the top commitments are getting attention. If the team is getting pulled into things that are not in the plan, escalate this to the attention of your boss. This does not mean refusing to do unplanned work (which would hardly be "agile"), but making sure that the roadmap doesn't drift away from reality and become useless. Instead, any gap between planned work and actual is new information to be fed back into the discussion and used to reset expectations and make intentional choices about new trade-offs.

- Each quarter, you should revisit the roadmap with all the stakeholders, review what was done, what has moved from Next to Now, what has moved from Later to Next, and what new ideas need to be tracked for Later.

Managing Expectations

There is no way to avoid the expectation that your team is going to ship certain promised features or solutions or fixes by committed deadlines. You should do your best to communicate that a roadmap deals with a series of time horizons that necessarily get vaguer and more speculative the farther out you go. Still, no matter how carefully you build and present your roadmap in ways to avoid looking like a Gantt chart, your stakeholders will still want to know when to expect the launch or next release.

Thematic roadmaps don't get you out of obligations.

They can help frame the conversation, though. When you present a roadmap covering time frames called Now, Next, and Later, and a stakeholder points to an item in the Next bucket and asks you when you expect the team to get to that, what do you say?

One thing you can do is map the horizons to approximate chunks of time. Here is an example that worked for me:

- **Now** refers to this quarter, a roughly 1–3 month period, depending on where you are in the quarter.

- **Next** is the six-month period following the current quarter. The items in that bucket will likely come to fruition in that period, but it's impossible to be more specific. (So at this point, the plan covers roughly 7–9 months.)

- **Later** is the nine-month period that takes you out to about a year and a half from the start of the current quarter. It's pretty much impossible to make plans farther out than 18 months, and the items you've parked in the second half of that time frame are necessarily broad and subject to revision every time you reevaluate your roadmap.

Beyond that, the best way to manage the expectations of the people looking to your roadmap as the best insight into what to expect from your team is to present roadmap updates and status reports to the larger organization on a regular basis, at least once a quarter and more frequently for the teams directly adjacent to your own.

Epilogue to the "Break-Even" Story

As you may recall from an anecdote in Chapter 8, "Getting the Money," a start-up for which I ran the product team, 7 Cups, managed to break even after a series of revenue experiments. If you want to know how things went *after* we hit breakeven, well that story hasn't really finished, although my part of it has come to an end, but I can fill in what happened next. At this point, we faced three paths:

- **Where we're going there are no roads:** Break-even business as a platform for experimentation

- **The band is just fantastic:** Doubling down on the value in the core service and the paid version of it

- **Go for broke:** Looking for breakthrough, game-changing, market-making opportunities

We started down path number two with a roadmap geared toward tightening up our offering, continuing to optimize our sign-up flow and subscription service, improving at scaling the paid service tier, and ultimately making enterprise deals with health and insurance providers better positioned to underwrite emotional support and gain the benefits of broader services than point-of-sale consumer transactions could ever accomplish.

Along the way, a shiny government innovation contract presented itself and tempted the business onto path three, searching for another radical breakthrough.

Sadly, around the time I left, that approach had fizzled out, and I fear there might have been a missed opportunity to scale the initial success, but the good news is that this has likely forced the current leadership to focus again on path no. 2, which still to my mind represents a winner.

The Art of Saying No

The hardest part of being the person who has to establish priorities is protecting them once the rubber meets the road. There will be an endless supply of requests—heartfelt, sincere requests—for a dispensation to add just one more special new thing to the roadmap. There will also be demands from people with more power than you. And there will be endless "suggestions" from folks whom you need to work with, but whose ideas you are not willing (or able) to put ahead of your real priorities.

Fielding and addressing these cross-pressures is demanding, especially when you're not the boss, and even a chief product officer must stand naked (metaphorically speaking) and defend priorities against a CEO or a board when whoever signs their paychecks demands due consideration for a fresh idea (even if that idea did come from a recent *Harvard Business Review* article the CEO's first-class seatmate summarized for them on the flight home from Cabo).

FROM THE TRENCHES...

GETTING TO YES

As a counterpoint, Matt LeMay pointed out a danger is this negative framing: "I see PMs fall in love with saying 'no' and miss out on critical information. From my point of view, the goal is to ask 'why' before you say 'yes' or 'no.' Whenever an exec comes to you with a new idea or somebody tries to override something, there's a reason behind that, and it's your job to understand that reason."

Who Will You Have to Say No To?

At various times, you may have to find a way to say no to any of a wide range of potential stakeholders, including:

- Customers
- Partners
- Advisors
- Sales, Business Development, Partners, and Customer Success
- Marketing
- Engineers
- UX Designers (sorry!)
- CEOs

And you can't blow these people off. You don't need to capitulate and let them disrupt your best-laid plans (most of the time), but you do need to give them the time of day.

Who Does Have a Say?

Ellen Chisa, a product leader and currently Founder-in-Residence at Boldstart Ventures, likes to note that there are four main inputs that contribute to your roadmap to varying degrees at different stages of product development (as in this talk on YouTube[1]):

1. The **product** vision
2. Feedback from **users**
3. What the **data** is telling you
4. **Ideas** that come from the rest of the team (bandwidth permitting)

That first slice in some scenarios is the "CEO features," but in an empowered product team, they are arising out of product strategy. Still, there is usually a CEO or equivalent in the picture, and there is no shame in accepting that they have a legitimate right to drive at least some portion of the roadmap, as the person ultimately responsible for the well-being of the enterprise and the execution of its strategy.

Nonetheless, saying no to the boss is still part of the job, as unpleasant as it may be in reality, and when the time comes for you to make the presentation, ideally you'll have practiced letting lower-level stakeholders down easy any number of times, to hone your tactics.

---

1   "Balance: Prioritizing Your Roadmap Across Product Stages" www.youtube.com/watch?v=udobV6mlGjg

Most of the time, the key to saying no is not to negate the value of the request or the significance of it for the requester. In fact, the best approach is something like this:

1. Thank the stakeholder for offering their advice.

2. Ask questions about the suggestion: What problem is it intended to solve or opportunity is it intended to exploit? What is the expected outcome of delivering this feature or ideas? What are the risks of not doing it? Were other ways to address this situation considered?

3. Offer to research and explore the problem space further.

4. Review the current top priorities in the Now bucket and how they connect to company strategy, objectives, and key results.

5. Ask which of the commitments that have already been presented, argued for, and have obtained buy-in should be set aside to pursue this new potential priority. Remind them that these changes will need to be reviewed and reevaluated by all stakeholders.

6. Ask for data to justify this priority and have your own data ready to make the case for the priorities you already fought for and won.

7. And, finally, if overpowered and forced to elevate an unwanted priority, be sure to define success metrics, measure the impact, and report back eventually, both on the eventual outcome of the novel idea, as well as the impact of dropping the priorities that had to be cut to make room.

By the way, sometimes the idea that the boss makes you do is a good one, and it turns out they were right. It's all part of the job.

When the Brass Wants Aha!

If you've gone down the road of a thematic, outcome-oriented roadmap with increasing time frames and have successfully avoided being forced to produce a list of features and ship dates under the heading "roadmap," you'll likely find that a product such as ProdPad is ideally suited to this approach. (It's no coincidence that one of their founders, Janna Bastow, has championed this model and influenced a generation of product managers in this direction.)

But this is not going to change the fact that your stakeholders will still want to know when new things are going to ship, and the executive types are quite likely to find ProdPad's presentation options somewhat hard to follow. The more complex your product portfolio, and the more strongly they are hoping for something like a Gantt chart, the more likely you may find yourself pressured into adopting (or at least "evaluating") another roadmap product, like Aha! (Figure 10.9).

FIGURE 10.9

If you have a complex roadmap and need to communicate it in multiple ways, a tool like Aha! can help (but it may drag you back into the "release plan vs. roadmap" battle all over again).

Aha! is powerful and provides many more dimensions of complexity than ProdPad does. Their model of products, projects, epics, and so on may not map perfectly to your product taxonomy, but it is fairly malleable and can be adapted to fit many complex environments.

It also offers the ability to maintain entirely separate views of your roadmap. This means you can, for example, make one version with strong presentation values for a marketing department slide deck or a sales presentation. At the same time, you can maintain an internal version of the roadmap that "lets it all hang out," including internal maintenance, technical debt, and other unglamorous priorities, and provides more working detail.

Ultimately, you need to be agnostic about tools and able to ply your trade with whatever kit prevails in your current shop. When you're the boss or building your own product org, you can own the exciting task of selecting which product operations tools will unleash the awesome potential of your team.

A DAY IN THE LIFE OF A SAAS PM

Ian Johnson, Principal/Director of Product at Flow Commerce, Inc.

What industry do you work in?

E-commerce

How mature (or how long established) is the organization you work for?

4 years, 70 people

Share anything else that might help describe the environment in which you practice product management:

SaaS products B2B

How do you start your workday?

Checking emails and Slack channels

How do you spend most of the morning?

Either reading up on key industry reports, customer data, or potentially responding to ad hoc requests

How does the morning end?

Daily stand-up

When do you take a lunch break?

About 12:30

What do you do first in the afternoon?

Meetings with stakeholders

How do you handle "fire drills" or other unplanned work?

Assess severity and then address based on the context

How do you spend the bulk of the afternoon?

In meetings

What do you do at the end of the workday?

Wrap up with focused work for a period of 1–2 hours

Do you work in the evening?

Almost always ■

Key Insights

- A roadmap communicates what goals the product team is working on now and planning to work on in the future.

- A roadmap is *not* a launch plan.

- Roadmaps are best managed in three time horizons: Now, Next, and Later.

- Roadmaps should focus on desired outcomes organized by themes, and not laundry lists of wish list features and pet peeves.

- A product roadmap communicates the product strategy, which is itself an expression of the organization's larger strategy.

- You may own an entire roadmap or just a tiny part of one.

- Roadmap planning requires rigorous, systematic prioritization of ideas that may come from vision, users, data, and colleagues.

- You'll need to make a case for your priorities and obtain buy-in for your roadmap.

- Roadmaps require constant care and feeding, and you need to keep stakeholders abreast of updates and changes as priorities evolve and external circumstances change.

- Practice saying *no*.

- The boss may still overrule you.

- It can be useful at times to be able to show your roadmap in multiple ways, depending on who is asking for it.

CHAPTER 11

Chief Information Architect

Depending on the size of the product team and its position in the organization, the leader of the team might have any number of different titles: chief product officer, vice president of product, director of product management, or even group product manager. Sometimes the title is just head of product, leaving the exact level ambiguous.

In some organizations the head of product or CPO has a design peer, a Chief Experience Officer (CXO) or Chief Design Officer (CDO), or Head of UX (or Design), but this structure is (sadly, for UXers) still more the exception than the rule. More often, both UX and product management ultimately roll up to be a head of product.

Thus, if you do choose to pursue a product management career founded on your UX expertise, then the promotion ladder will potentially take you to a product leadership role, where you may find yourself (once again) managing designers alongside product managers and likely some other skill sets as well (data science and analysis, customer success, maybe even some engineers).

The Head of Product's Secret Sauce

When the internet first took off, the people doing what we now call *user experience strategy, research, and design* were called *information architects*. Over time, new roles and titles came along (*interaction designer, UX designer, product designer*) and the role of an IA was gradually reduced to either "figuring out the navigation" for websites or limited to information-rich environments that needed the library-science skills of taxonomy, ontology, synonym rings, and the rest.

But along the way, information architecture also reasserted itself as a discipline in its own right with important things to say about notions of space, embodiment, information, and wayfinding. As discussed in earlier chapters, the IA practices of mapping systems to reveal their concepts and meaning and providing a coherent picture and story about what the team is actually building turn out to be crucial skills to bring to bear in product management at every level.

Years ago, when I was working for one of my product mentors, Matte Scheinker, in an attempt to reboot AOL (now finally absorbed into Yahoo and sold off to private equity by Verizon), I told him I was surprised that we didn't have any information architects on staff, as it wasn't even a job title in the HR system anymore.

Matte (pronounced "mott-ee") turned to me and asked, "Well, how many IAs does a company need?" So I thought about that question before answering and then said, "At least one."

This got me thinking that somebody in the company needs to be the chief information architect to do the hard work of mapping the problem/opportunity space and the meaning and purpose of the product in that larger system.

There are many organizations where nobody does this work for the product or portfolio as a whole, even if lots of really good UX designers and PMs are thinking intelligently about the IA and structure of their specific features and projects. If anyone is telling that larger story, it tends to be the head of product (or sometimes, for sure, a head of design).

Someone needs to take responsibility for the coherence of the product at the highest level. Information architect and consultant Jorge Arango put it this way in his *Informed Life* podcast in 2020:[1]

> Where within this [product management] framework is there a place for looking after the coherence between those things? Especially if they're part of some kind of ecosystem or family of products. Eventually those things need to cohere at some level....

> My favorite example of the lack of such a thing is Kindle. I've been using Kindle for a while to read books, so I should be familiar with it. And I use Kindle in three very different device platforms. I have a dedicated Kindle reader. I have Kindle on my iOS devices, iPad and iPhone. And I also use Kindle on my Mac, and I find things like navigation structures to be different in all three.

This "decoherence" among versions of the same product is a consequence of fragmented pressures from different platforms, tech stacks, and user bases.

There are natural tensions even when trying to impose a consistent paradigm across a family of related products. Individual teams will object, saying "Yeah, but that doesn't work for my device," or, "But I have reasons for this," or "It's always been this way on our subplatform. You bought us and now you're trying to make us be part of you."

---

1 "Christian Crumlish on Product Management" https://theinformed.life/2020/03/01/episode-30-christian-crumlish/

Where everything is constantly shifting, especially in a larger organization, it's almost impossible to impose coherence from the top down, but a product leader can gradually bring a complex system into harmony. As Dawn Russell, who is an information architect at CVS Health, said:

> I would argue decoherence is also born from org structure and internal funding models, especially in companies/products where many lines of business live under one brand. For example, at CVS Health, we offer flu shots through both the pharmacy and our MinuteClinic. Same shot, same topic, even same location, but different lines of business. So without a chief architect that "looks across" these lines of business to drive coherence, we've ended up with two ways to schedule a flu shot on one domain, placing the onus on the customer to navigate and understand.

It often seems that every big organization is literally either in the process of becoming a little bit more decentralized or a little bit more centralized, or it's finished doing one of those things and it's about to start doing the other one. They never find the perfect amount of decentralization and centralization, so you get matrix reporting. People end up with both a boss and a practice leader, and during reorgs they vibrate between reporting to one or the other primarily. Unfortunately, this kind of organizational thrash also tends to produce product experiences that are all over the map.

Ideally, you are shooting for a holistic UX instead of a unique experience for each expression of your product. That means that you don't do the UX of your Kindle on the Mac and the UX of your Kindle on the Kindle and your UX of the Kindle on iOS, and the UX of the Kindle on Android devices, and so on, each as separate exercises managed by siloed teams.

Kindle should have one UX, and Kindle should have an information architecture that is one big map. And then everything should be some articulation of that or some expression of that. There will be compromises, but there should always be a larger sense of unity and cohesion. Without someone in product leadership focusing on this goal and working toward it, drift is inevitable.

Be a Boss

For years, UX fought for "a seat at the table," or to be in the room where it happens. Along the way, people started forming product organizations, and it seemed that most UX jobs had a reporting structure that eventually reached someone in a product role. To get a seat at the boss's table, it could feel like you needed to be a product leader.

Now that is changing somewhat, to some extent, and in some contexts. There are design executives and organizations where product and UX design sit together as peers at the very highest level of the org chart, but in either scenario, all roles converge at the leadership level. Whether you come in the door wearing a product hat or a design badge, you sit down together and come to decisions about product and organization strategy together around the same table. You each bring your expertise and the ability of your team to deliver to that table, but by the time you get there it might not matter as much to you which door you came in.

Then again, in many organizations, the top dog in the shared space of product and UX still has a product title. This is not the best reason to choose product over design at the fork in your career road, but it is a legitimate consideration. If your organization needs product leadership, if it needs an information architect mapping and clarifying the product roadmap, why shouldn't that boss be you?

Just remember that once you climb that pinnacle, get a seat at the table, and have a voice in the direction of your product, all the most difficult decisions are going to come to your desk, and it's going to be you who is awake at 3 a.m. remembering problems nobody else is worrying about (Figure 11.1).

FIGURE 11.1
Be careful what you wish for! By the time you become the boss of product, you inherit all the biggest problems and all the riskiest decisions.

LEARNING TO SPEAK EXECUTIVE

Harry Max is a leadership consultant who has guided many product and UX leaders. He points out that designers are often not all that great at communicating with executives.

"If you want to be taken seriously and you want a seat at the table and you want to start dealing with executives, you have to start speaking the language of business. You've got to talk about making money. You've got to talk about saving money. You've got to talk about avoiding unnecessary costs."

You've got to talk about building brand, building market share, hiring and retaining talent, and identifying, pursuing, and executing goals and objectives. You've got to figure out how to make progress day in and day out, period, and you really have to step outside yourself and start looking at how you're communicating.

"It starts with speaking the language of the people that you're interacting with. And if you're doing it in a for-profit environment and you're doing it in a business, you really have to use the language of business. And if you're doing it in a civic-oriented environment, you've got to start using the language of policy, the language of constituents.

"You have to get inside the head of the people. UX people often speak the language of design and visuals and information architecture and usability. Leaders are trying to figure out how to steer an organization in a direction. They're responsible for people, they're responsible for projects, and they're responsible for money. They've got lots of constituents, whether they're investors or bankers or whoever.

"Your listening skills have to shift. You'll have to discern things at a higher level of abstraction. You have to get beyond active listening and move into what I characterize as *deep listening.*

"The higher you go, the more the people you're communicating with will work to move a conversation forward, because they are discovering what they want to learn as you're talking. This means that when they're asking you questions, you have to answer the questions they're asking, not the ones you were trying to answer yourself. You're answering very precisely, and you're anticipating to some extent where they might want to go so that you can be efficient about helping them get there, but you're not telling stories!

"You're not giving these long preambles and you're not giving a lot of excuses and it's not because they don't want to hear excuses, which they don't, but it has to do with the fact that what they're really trying to do is get to something that's meaningful and interesting. That helps move the conversation forward for them.

"So precision questioning and answering and deep listening are critical, too. I think it's especially true of designers who are interested in pursuing more responsibility and higher level goals, because the expectation is already there that they're good at it. And if they don't do it, they're being downgraded for it.

"It's going to boil down to: Are you in a position to make clear the requests, and accept and deliver on agreements that you've made? Can you draw a through-line from a thought to a conversation to an action, to a decision, to a request, to an agreement? Do you understand the outcome frame around that? That is, what does success actually look like and how do you clarify it for yourself and for others?

"How do you avoid tacit agreements? 'Hey, I realized that when we were talking about this, that, you know, you asked me to do something and I needed time to think about it, but I just realized that you probably left with the impression that I'm actually going to do this, and I don't even know when you want it done.'"

Selling Your Team's Services Internally as a Product

One of the most reliable forms of advice an experienced practitioner can give an up-and-coming UXer is to apply their user-centered research and design "superpowers" to more problems than just the design of interfaces and software product experiences in general.

As you progress in this world of collaborative technology development, you will notice along the way that the difference between success and failure often has a lot more to do with "soft skills," team performance, and interpersonal dynamics than the tech stack or navigation paradigm you choose.

UX SUPERPOWER ALERT
WHEN THE PRODUCT IS INNOVATION ITSELF

If you've ever had to sell UX in an organization new to it or re-luctant to embrace it, then you've seen that arrogant evangelism backfires, but that deeply understanding the needs of your users, er, colleagues, reflecting on the "usability" of your deliverables and communications, and crafting an experience (of working with you) that delights, relieves pain, and solves real problems is the path to success.

The same "advice" trick applies to job searches and getting bet-ter at interviewing. Take all your abilities to understand people's needs, motivations, worries and fears, and to shape experiences designed to address those needs and apply them to the experi-ence of hiring you. Lather, rinse, repeat.

So it is with product management, where the disciplines of obsessing intensely about the unmet needs and aspirations of your "customer," crafting a solution that addressed the demands of a "market," and packaging your services as a "product" can be turned to other goals beyond enticing people to complete transactions.

The state of California's Office of Digital Innovation, for example, does build and ship digital software products in the sense that most people mean. For example, the team built the state's pandemic response website (**covid19.ca.gov**), shown in Figure 11.2, a new site for the state's cannabis licensing authorities (**cannabis.ca.gov**), and another special site to help the state's public conserve water (**drought.ca.gov**).

FIGURE 11.2
California's Office of Digital Innovation (ODI) spun up the **covid19.ca.gov** site in response to the pandemic to provide the state's public and government officials with a single reliable source of current guidance and information.

Those websites can be thought of as products in a more-or-less-traditional sense, despite the lack of any commercial transactions or consumer goals (though the cannabis site will enable license applications). The deeper mission of the innovation team is to help enable all of the state's agencies to produce highly performant, very usable websites that communicate in plain language and make data open and accessible.

For this goal, the "product" is more a set of beneficial practices and some tools and services (such as a design system and consulting resources), and the "customers" are colleagues in adjacent state agencies. Here again, the product management's deep curiosity about the needs of the person they are trying to serve, rapid iteration through a build/measure/learn cycle, and thoughtful communication, illustration, and storytelling enable them to meet the demands of this internal "market."

Frankly, all teams need to do a certain amount of this, persuasion of other teams and leaders as to the value of their skills and talents and offerings. It's just that the UX and product superpowers are particularly helpful when you train the lens on your surroundings as well as your external markets.

Overcommunicate Deliberately

Fundamentally, successful alignment within a larger organization comes down to communication, making sure that the work your team does is "legible" (clear to read, and easy to understand), always staying ahead of changing circumstances to keep expectations current, and overcommunicating wherever possible.

For example, if you lead a product team, you should plan a regular cadence of sharing updates on the product roadmap, showcases of the work currently underway, and retrospective analyses of the outcomes from what was shipped in the past.

Partner with the Voice of the Customer

It's shocking how many organizations keep their customers at arm's length. Even when there are teams dedicated to supporting or otherwise interacting with customers, they are often siloed off away from the rest of the organization and treated more like a cost center than as an invaluable source of research, let alone the external nervous system of the org itself.

Years ago, Craig Newmark, founder of Craigslist, made a point of focusing on customer support instead of making himself CEO of his own business. He made a strong case that the only way for a collective entity such as a business or enterprise to actually learn and evolve is to channel feedback from external signals directly to the decision-making center. He championed empowering customer support professionals to report what they were hearing and to propose solutions.

Whatever the prevailing culture you find yourself in, part of your mission will be to forge ties with customer support, customer success, and community managers. These people can offer you solid gold insights into what your customers and larger community of supporters want, need, talk about, complain about, love, hate, and trend toward.

Any product success I've ever had has derived at least in part from close collaboration with customer support and community managers, leveraging their access and analyses to form a deeper and richer picture of where the product needs to go, and even working directly with customers in the product's community, gathering their wishes and feedback, sharing early design sketches with them, recruiting beta testers, and enlisting supporters to help spread the word.

Building Product Teams

Once you're running a product team, you're in the business of hiring and building the strengths of that team. Creating a strong product organization starts with a commitment from the top, and now this will mean you.

Change is never easy and new habits cause friction when they clash with comforting older customs. Your executive championship of the product mindset will be a necessary, but not sufficient, ingredient in transforming your business and empowering your product people.

Define the skills your product team needs to bring to bear, make some skills histograms (as explained in Chapter 3, "UX Skills That Carry Over"), and start recruiting to hire people who can help your team level up in the critical areas where you are not collectively strong enough yet. Also, look for the product people who are currently in other roles. Some will be participatory allies and part of the product culture you are hoping to grow, and others may be great candidates to move over to the product track under a leader who can help mentor someone through such a change.

Enable Transitions

When you are growing a product team out of the "soil" of your existing staff, you will want to identify people who show the sort of aptitude and instincts discussed throughout this book. They may be engineers, designers, marketers, business analysts, project managers, sales people, customer support staff, or really anyone.

Make it clear that you are building a product practice, and that it will involve some hiring. Explain that people in other roles will also be involved, as the entire enterprise takes on the habits of a product organization. Finally, be sure to welcome people formally transitioning into product management roles from their existing jobs and facilitate this by providing training, coaching, and mentorship.

A DAY IN THE LIFE OF A VP OF PRODUCT

Benoît des Ligneris, Vice President of Product at Woolf

Share anything else that might help describe the environment in which you practice product management.

Hyper-growth industry with lots of innovation and competition.

How do you spend the early morning?

Waking up with the sun, meditating 20 minutes, chores, strength training/ bike ride/run, walk 30–45 minutes, and then work from home.

How do you start your workday?

By a 30-minute walk outside to plan my day and solve problems or define goals.

How do you spend most of the morning?

I do not have a typical morning! I have lots of meetings and try to get them early in the week.

Monday–Tuesday morning is when I tend to have my key meetings outside of the product team.

Wednesday is a "no meeting" day: only craft-based activities (to become a better PM, not to PM something...) in the morning.

Thursday: Recruiting and peers.

Friday: This is when I have my meeting with senior leadership, I try to focus on this.

How does the morning end?

Noon. I have it in my agenda: no meeting during lunch time. Especially working from home, it is important to have boundaries and key rituals in place. Most of the time, this is a meeting with someone from my team. I like the idea to wish folks "bon appétit" and share some detail about our daily lives.

When do you take a lunch break?

Noon. I typically spend 30 minutes to eat and then go for a walk outside (whether -30 C or +45) with my wife: Non-negotiable "us time."

What do you do first in the afternoon?

Lots of key meetings with other teams and customer sessions tend to start at 1 p.m. sharp. Everyone is quite productive after lunch.

How do you handle "fire drills" or other unplanned work?

My limits for a productive Monday are between 7–12 meetings as I try to gather key information for the week. Plus, I try to book all my extra meetings on Monday so that I can organize my week around this new information. The other days, my schedule is lighter with 4–8 meetings maximum. Because Wednesday is a "no meeting day," it nicely cuts the week in half and helps create some slack in my schedule.

How do you spend the bulk of the afternoon?

Being a morning person, I am less productive in the afternoon, and I tend to keep it for the more tedious work—work that is automatic, or that I enjoy less, in particular:

- reporting
- status update
- checking KPI
- updating documents/iterating on feedback

What do you do at the end of the workday?

I also do my best to stop at 5 p.m. sharp. It does not happen all the time as lots of candid conversations tend to happen at the end of the workdays—especially for my reports. Lots of the emergencies also require a kind of end-of-day check-in to align for the next day. Those are the two occasions I allow myself to work past 5 p.m.

Do you work in the evening?

Occasionally. ■

Investing in Your Team

You should constantly look for ways to develop your team's product craft. Product people need to master the skills and techniques discussed throughout this book, and you need to help them do that. Product leadership needs to put in place the educational opportunities and events, the training programs, and an operation that provides career growth and professional development for product practitioners.

Product training should be offered to any practitioner who is interested, not just to people with product manager job titles. The goal is to nurture and validate a product mindset in any role, across the entire organization (Figure 11.3).

FIGURE 11.3

Atlassian puts on an internal product craft conference annually to train product people and build the product practice community across the company.

Cross-Training for Increased Fitness

A reliable way to broaden and strengthen product skills across your org is through cross-training. This depends on having at least one person who has mastered the skill that others are hoping to develop. Let's take, for example, the practice of tracking product analytical data, such as retention and working systematically to improve it.

This proficiency involves a handful of techniques and skills that can be learned, among them:

- Capturing valid meaningful data
- Manipulating charts and graphs to analyze the data
- Engaging in discovery to understand what is going on with customers that might explain the data
- Developing hypotheses about what might improve the experience
- Prioritizing experiments to test these hypotheses
- Learning from the outcomes of experiments and feeding this learning back into the discovery process

The best way to cross-train a product person who is more junior or who has less experience with these activities is to pair them with a senior product person who excels at these things. The key part is that the person who is learning does the work. The person who has the wisdom and experience provides coaching, guidance, and feedback.

In the short term, these tasks will take a bit longer than if they were assigned to the experienced hand, but the benefit in distributing this expertise more widely across the team outweighs this cost, and the more that cross-training goes on, the more supple and agile the product team will be—more able to flex, recombine, and adapt to handle changing circumstances.

Someone Has to Lead—Why Not You?

Remember, whatever path you decide is right for you, every effort you're part of is going to need someone to be that chief information architect, whether that's the head of product, the head of product's design right-hand thought partner, or the head of design. It all comes together at the top.

Key Insights

- Information architecture can be a unique superpower for a product lead.
- Whether you become a PM or stay a UX designer in a product world, you can still get a seat at the table.
- As a product leader, one of your products is your team—its customers are your colleagues, and its market is your organization.
- Make sure that your work is legible and you overcommunicate.
- Product leadership means building the scaffolding for the development of more product talent.
- Be a boss.

INDEX

breaking even, 131, 133–135, 143, 144–145, 181–182

Breaking into Product Management (Kao), 83

broken glass (hard test), 120, 124. *See also* crawling through glass

Brunckhorst, Janet, 105

bucket testing, 108, 116. *See also* A/B testing

buggy software, 60–61

Build, Measure, Learn cycle, 12–13, 55, 168, 198

build phase of development, and experimentation, 109

bullying, and help from 7 Cups, 134

burndown charts, 57–58

business

    language of, 194–195

    multiple lines of, 145

business managers, 6–8

business of product, 69–86

    building sustainable value, 70

    business operations, 81–82

    business-to-business (B2B) products, 83

    customer obsession, 79–80

    financial business skills, 82–83

    finding product-market fit, 74–77

    go-to-market plan, 77–79

    launching vs. optimizing, 80–81

    targeting a market, 71–74

    thinking of the market, 70–71

    typical day of enterprise PM, 84–85

business operations, 81–82

business-to-business (B2B)

    A/B tests in enterprise contexts, 120

    customers and users, 83, 84

    revenue models, 131

business-to-business-to-consumer (B2B2C), 83

business-to-consumer (B2C), 83

business-to-government (B2G), 83

C

cadences, 53–56

Cagan, Marty, 11–12

California's Office of Digital Innovation, 196–198

cannabis website, 196, 198

career reasons to become a PM, 19–20

Cartesian plot, for prioritizing roadmap, 174–175

centralization and decentralization in organization, 192

CEOs

    compared with product managers, 7

    input on roadmap, 183–184

    language of executives, 194–195

chief information architect, 189–204

    be the boss, 193, 203

    building product teams, 199–200

    coherence across product family, 190–192

    cross-training, 202–203

    executive language, 194–195

    investing in the team, 201–203

    selling team services internally as a product, 196–199

    typical day of VP of Product, 200–201

    UX skill of information architecture, 43–45

chief product officer (CPO), 190

Chisa, Ellen, 183

Christensen, Clay, 146

churn, 98

Cleveland, Dirk, 152

CloudOn, 3, 73, 78–79

co-design (co-creation) session, 67

coefficient of virality, 102–103

Coforma, 66

coherence across product family, 190–192

in the org chart, 157–158

overlap of skills and conflicts, 150–152

service design, 160

production fires. *See* "fire drills"

professional reasons to become a PM, 19–20

profit and loss (P&L)

ownership of product, 82

in product's lifecycle, 130–131

program management, 81

program managers, 7

project management, 81

project management tools, 57–59

project managers, 4

prototypes, 123

proxy metrics, 104

Psychology Today (magazine), 140–141

Q

qualitative research, 74

quarterly planning, 54

questions

asking smart ones, 65

precision, in language of executives, 195

R

Ramen profitable, 144–145

Ramirez, Kristen, 160

reach, in RICE framework, 178

Redfern, Joff, 8

referral, 96, 102–103

release plans

as opposed to roadmap, 12, 165–166, 168, 180, 185

waiting too long, 34

research

qualitative, 74

in targeting a market, 72

research and design, relationship with product management and engineering, 153

research/launch cycle, 46

respect, giving to and earning from engineers, 63–65

retention, 96, 99–102, 143

retrospective meetings, 62–63

return on investment (ROI), in UX design, 130

revenue. *See also* money

in customer lifecycle, 96, 97, 103

lifecycle of product, 131, 145–147

models, 131–133

RICE (reach, impact, confidence, and effort) framework, 172–173, 178

Ries, Eric, 12

roadmaps, 163–187

art of saying "no," 182–185

company objectives, 169–170

defined, 164–165

epilogue to "break-even" story, 181–182

expectations management, 180–181

horizons: Now, Next, Later, 12, 53, 166–168, 180–181

monthly review, 53–54, 180

as opposed to launch plans, 12, 78, 165, 166, 180

outcomes, 12, 168–169

ownership of, 170–171

populating and maintaining, 179–181

prioritization, 171–178. *See also* prioritization on roadmap

product strategy, 168–171

themes and goals, 169

typical day of SaaS PM, 186

rough consensus, 156

Rumsey, Ryan, 125, 126

Russell, Dawn, 192

venture capitalists, 134–135

"viral" as metaphor, 103

viral coefficient, 102–103

Vohra, Rahul, 76–77

"Volunteer as a Listener," 110

W

water conservation website, 196

WAU (weeky active users), 98

websites of innovation, 196–198

weekly retention analysis, 100

white label, as revenue generating experiment, 139–140

Whysel, Noreen, 82

Williams, Maisie, 134

Wizard of Oz test, 120, 122–123

Woolf, 200

Word on the iPad, 73, 78–79, 124

working agreements, 156

writing, as task of PM, 25, 36, 49

Wroblewski, Luke, 19

Y

Yahoo

Developer Network, concept model as poster, 44

producers, 11

product team promotions, 19

user experience design at, xvii–xviii

YCombinator, 75, 133

yearly planning, 54–55

Z

Zappos, Wizard of Oz testing, 123

Zaveri, Jay, 3, 73, 78–79, 124

ACKNOWLEDGMENTS

So many people have helped me both literally write this book and also to develop the material over the past several years. Both one-on-one chats and threaded conversations in the Design in Product community helped persuade me that a book like this could reach a growing cohort of product-curious UXers, design-sensitive product managers, and product leaders with a firm foundation in user-centered research and design.

To start with, I have been blessed with some stellar product mentors, advisors, wise compadres, and sounding boards over the years, especially Christina Wodtke, Matte Scheinker, Jay Zaveri, Rich Mironov, Laura Klein, Ellen Chisa, Matt LeMay, Hà Phan, Tom Kerwin, and Angelica Quirarte. Ken Norton has been especially kind to me at several key junctures in my career path.

A cluster of folks who opened doors for me or shaped my thinking along the way (Erin Malone, Dorelle Rabinowitz, Larry Cornett, Bryce Glass, Kent Brewster, Nam Nguyen, Havi Hoffman, Laurie Voss, and others I am no doubt forgetting) came into my life through Yahoo, and we recently lost a giant among that cohort, the legendary Bill W. Scott. He was a mentor and a friend and the internet will miss him.

Jeff Lash, Chris Baum, Jeff Gothelf, and Josh Seiden all helped at critical moments to open up my development into a product management leader.

Some of the above folks, along with many others, made their time available to me for one or more interviews, or provided an example of a day in the life of a product manager, including Bibiana Nunes, Noreen Whysel, Peter Boersma, Madonnalisa Chan, Dawn Russell, Alëna Iouguina, Clement Kao, Marvin Cheung, Ana Giraldo-Wingler, Harry Max, B. Pagels-Minor, Kristen Ramirez, Sara Menefee, Brent Palmer, Michael Curry, Janet Brunckhorst, Benoît des Ligneris, Ian Johnson, Nicholas Duran, and Adam Connor.

Quite a few folks from the Design in Product community read early chapters of this book or otherwise contributed ideas and resources to the material. (You can join this community yourself, if you wish. Just drop by designinproduct.typeform.com/to/H4PqHsVE and introduce yourself.) These people include (and I apologize if I am overlooking anyone) Jenn Downs, Ryan Rumsey, Bogdan Stanciu, Felipe Delgado, Austin Govella, Erin Stratos, Boon Sheridan, Shelby Bower, Jake Krajewski, Chris Chandler, David LaCroix, Jo Ho, Jeppe Kruse, Brad Peters, Rebecca Bar, Tania Schlatter, Lukas Bergstrom, Brian Durkin, Iga Gawronska, Vinish Garg, and Christopher Filkins.

Any mistakes or errors in judgment in this book are mine and mine alone.

Rosenfeld Media is my kind of publisher, incorporating user research, strategy, and design into the bones of each book. I was overjoyed when I realized the topic I had in mind for this book might be a great fit for their list. I still remember sidling up to Lou Rosenfeld at my first Information Architecture Summit, in 2006, to introduce myself, and today I am proud to consider Lou a friend as well as a colleague. What a treat to get to work with your heroes and friends!

Everyone I've worked with at Rosenfeld is top-notch. Karen Corbett is a wonderful operations manager. Adeline Crites-Moore takes an approach to marketing that is in perfect harmony with the ethos of the press. Jason Shuler takes a thoughtful and inquisitive approach to social media, imagine that! Danielle Foster did an amazing job laying this book out. Seriously, flip through the pages and tell me I'm wrong. She also turned my scribbly stick-figure illustrations into well-mannered images and diagrams that perfectly complement the text. The critical work of indexing (Marilyn Augst) and proofreading (Sue Boshers) a book often get taken for granted, but they are what distinguish a high-quality reading experience from the sort of stuff you can find for free everywhere you look. Thank them both!

The astounding, perfect cover art is by Heads of State. I want a full-sized print!

My editor, Marta Justak, is the gold standard. She sets the bar. I don't think I've ever had an editor so in tune with my voice, so able to encourage me when I needed it, and nudge me along when I felt stuck. I literally watched this book turn from a messy stream of consciousness under her hands into the well-wrought narrative you hold today. Every author should be so lucky.

 **Rosenfeld®**

Dear Reader,

Thanks very much for purchasing this book. There's a story behind it and every product we create at Rosenfeld Media.

Since the early 1990s, I've been a User Experience consultant, conference presenter, workshop instructor, and author. (I'm probably best-known for having cowritten *Information Architecture for the Web and Beyond*.) In each of these roles, I've been frustrated by the missed opportunities to apply UX principles and practices.

I started Rosenfeld Media in 2005 with the goal of publishing books whose design and development showed that a publisher could practice what it preached. Since then, we've expanded into producing industry-leading conferences and workshops. In all cases, UX has helped us create better, more successful products—just as you would expect. From employing user research to drive the design of our books and conference programs, to working closely with our conference speakers on their talks, to caring deeply about customer service, we practice what we preach every day.

Please visit **rosenfeldmedia.com** to learn more about our **conferences**, **workshops**, **free communities**, and **other great resources** that we've made for you. And send your ideas, suggestions, and concerns my way: louis@rosenfeldmedia.com

I'd love to hear from you, and I hope you enjoy the book!

Lou Rosenfeld,
Publisher